The Part and Parcel Murders

By the same author

One Was Not Enough
Motive to Murder
The Evil that Men Do
With Malice Aforethought
The Passion Killers
For Love of Money
Murders Unspeakable

The Part and Parcel Murders

GEORGINA LLOYD

ROBERT HALE · LONDON

ISBN 0 7090 4956 0

Robert Hale Limited
Clerkenwell House
Clerkenwell Green
London EC1R 0HT

Photoset in North Wales by
Derek Doyle & Associates, Mold, Clwyd.
Printed in Great Britain by
St Edmundsbury Press Ltd, Bury St Edmunds, Suffolk.
Bound by WBC Bookbinders Ltd, Bridgend, Mid-Glamorgan.

Contents

Introduction   7

1   **The Torso in the Marshes**
     Donald Hume (1949)   11
2   **The Brighton Trunk Murders**
     Unsolved (1934)   25
3   **The Tale of a Duck**
     Frederick Thorne (1897)   41
4   **Death of a Bag Lady**
     Robert Lee (1987)   47
5   **The Black Dahlia**
     Unsolved (1947)   61
6   **Draw the Well Dry**
     Pierre Voirbo (1869)   69
7   **The Bad Neighbour**
     Louis Voisin (1917)   79
8   **A Shock for the Plumber**
     Dennis Nilsen (1983)   85
9   **The Misbegotten**
     Albert Fish (1928)   105
10   **Folie à Deux**
     Douglas Clark and Carol Bundy (1983)   143
11   **A Quarter Million Dollars Bail**
     Richard Cottingham (1979)   155
12   **Mark of the Vampire**
     Richard Chase (1978)   165

Introduction

Murders in which the victims' bodies are dismembered are very rare, statistically speaking, when compared to those in which the victims are spared this final indignity. There are several reasons for this.

First of all, while the average murderer has no qualms about shooting, strangling, stabbing or bludgeoning his victim to death, he does draw the line at cutting up the body. He may be just squeamish; after all, he rationalizes to himself, the victim is dead, and butchering the corpse will not make it any more so. He also very quickly realizes another point: the dismemberment of a human body is a very difficult job, requiring a sound knowledge of human anatomy and a surgeon's skill at knowing exactly where to cut through connective tissues to disarticulate bones at the joints. Even a chicken is difficult to joint if you do not know precisely how and where to cut. Faced with this realization, even a killer who has considered the idea is unlikely to embark on this course if he has not the requisite know-how. All he would end up with would be a very messy job involving even more of a disposal problem than he had already.

For disposal is usually the name of the game. Murderers do not usually cut up bodies just for fun (although there have been a few notable exceptions, as we shall see); they do it to enable them to dispose of their problem more easily. It will not go away of itself; it will just lie there where it fell. It may well be too heavy to carry or drag outside to his car, even if rolled in a carpet. Besides, someone might easily spot him and wonder why he was doing it.

Yes (so his thinking goes), it will be much easier to cut up the body and get rid of a bit at a time. A black plastic garbage bag will hold a small torso (or half a large one), or a pair of legs or arms; a head will fit into an average size supermarket carton. The murderer can slip out with this kind of thing even in broad daylight and drop it into someone else's dustbin (a favoured method) or leave it on deserted waste ground, perhaps strewn over with rubbish to delay discovery, or in a wooded area, covered with leaves and bracken. Saves all the bother of grave-digging.

Now our murderer comes up against another snag. In order to dismember a body, bones must be sawn through. A power saw would do the job quickly enough, but it does make a great deal of noise, which would attract unwelcome attention, especially if the killer was not a man known to use power saws in the course of his work, or as a DIY enthusiast. Well, there's always a handsaw, but as well as taking considerably longer to do the job, sawing through bones even without benefit of power assistance is still a very noisy business. Small wonder, then, that so few murderers cut up their victims' bodies. They will find them much more difficult to dispose of in one piece, but that's their problem.

Another point sometimes overlooked is the blood. Blood traces are notoriously difficult to eradicate, and can be forensically detected, using sophisticated modern methods, months, or even years, after they have been deposited. Some murderers have not seemed to realize that a dead body does not bleed, since the heart has stopped pumping the blood around, and so they set to work dismembering it far too soon. These are the killers most likely to be caught sooner or later, not by the discovery of the remains, but betrayed by the bloodstains in unaccustomed places, which their most strenuous efforts failed to wash away completely.

This book tells the story of various murderers who did not let these pitfalls daunt them.

Georgina Lloyd
November 1992

1

The Torso in the Marshes

Donald Hume (1949)

On 21 October 1949 a wildfowler named Sidney Tiffin was in one of the loneliest parts of the Essex marshes, his gun and his game-bag slung over his shoulder. It had been a long walk from his home to reach Tillingham, on the estuary of the River Crouch. The mudflats were uncannily silent; the wind had dropped, and there was an eerie stillness in the air, broken only occasionally by a curlew's cry. Tiffin gazed out across the reed-beds and raised his gun, intending with the sound of a reverberating shot to flush out some duck. As he took aim, his glance happened to fall momentarily on the expanse of mud a little way before him. There, caught in some rushes, was a bundle which appeared to be some object wrapped in a covering of felt-like material, and tied together with cord. He decided to investigate. Laying his gun and bag down on a dry spot, he walked towards the bundle.

Gingerly he touched the bundle, which was soft and yielding beneath his fingers. Pushing aside the cord to look more closely and see what the package held, he quickly regretted his curiosity as the felt covering fell to one side, revealing to his horrified gaze a half-naked male torso, partly clad in the tattered remains of a silk shirt and underpants.

Stifling an urge to be sick, Tiffin made fast the bundle by hooking the cord with which it was fastened to a wooden stake, and left post-haste to find the nearest policeman. Not only would he and his family have no roast duck for supper, but he himself would not feel like eating any supper of any kind that night ...

For some reason the killer of the unidentified middle-aged man had cut off the head and legs but not the arms, and it was not long before the identity of the torso was known from the fingerprints. At New Scotland Yard the top fingerprint expert, Detective Chief Superintendent Fred Cherrill, was able to employ a recently developed technique for taking fingerprints from bodies which had been immersed in water for a considerable time, as this one had. This technique consisted of taking sections from the tips of the fingers, treating them with certain chemical reagents, and then transferring the sections to the fingertips of rubber gloves worn by the operator, which he would then fingerprint in the normal way. Police were able to identify the torso very quickly once they had the fingerprints, because they matched those of a known criminal on their books.

The victim was Stanley Setty, a 46-year-old professional car thief, black marketeer and 'spiv'. He was of Middle Eastern extraction, born in Baghdad and his name had originally been Sulman Seti. His parents had emigrated to the UK in 1907 with their family, and the boy's name had been changed to Stanley Setty. By 1928 he had already served fifteen months' imprisonment for various offences including currency frauds, car thefts, receiving stolen property and other offences of this kind. By 1949 he had amassed considerable funds and was able to reside in a sumptuously appointed flat in Regent's Park, London. During the Second World War he made vast profits from black market currency deals, and after the war ended returned to one of his favourite occupations – stealing cars and 'laundering' them for resale.

The police had no knowledge of who could have killed him, but they had a shrewd idea that it must have been someone who was in some way involved with him in these transactions and who stood to gain a large sum of money by his death. In the event they were proved right in their suppositions, but it had come about in a very different manner from what they had surmised.

Professor F.E. Camps, assisted by Dr Donald Teare, performed the post-mortem on the torso. Their findings were that death had been caused by shock and haemorrhage from multiple stab wounds to the chest and stomach, from which the victim would have died within minutes. Camps stated that, in his opinion, these wounds had been caused about forty-eight hours before the body had been put into the sea, and that this disposal had occurred at least two weeks, possibly longer, before it was washed up by the tide on the remote Essex mudflats where it had been found. Speculation now ensued as to how the torso had been put into the sea and at what point, and what had happened to the head and legs, which were never found. It seemed obvious that the head had been cut off to avoid identification, and the legs in order to facilitate the dumping of the remains. What the killer had not realized was that fingerprints were now able to be taken from a long-immersed, sodden body ...

Professor Camps provided the police with their first lead when he said that, in his opinion, the torso had been dropped from a height. The two Scotland Yard men conducting the investigation, Colin Macdougal and John Jamieson, thought that it could either have been dropped from a cliff, or dropped from an aeroplane. The cliff theory was untenable, since there were no cliffs in the area from which a body could have floated out and been washed up at the particular spot where it had been found. That left the aircraft theory, and it was this that led to the breakthrough in the case.

Stanley Setty had been last seen alive on 4 October, when he was known to have clinched a £1,000 car deal. Having after this transaction vanished from sight, he was reported missing by a group of his friends and colleagues who suspected that he could have been kidnapped or even murdered in furtherance of robbery. Forty odd years ago, one thousand pounds was a large sum of money.

During the course of inquiries by police officers, some of Setty's associates were traced in the course of police delving into the stolen car network which operated in the Warren Street area of London at that time. The area is still the centre of the used-car trade, though these days it is more above-board.

One of the missing man's associates in this shady trade was one Brian Donald Hume, a 39-year-old ex-RAF aircraftman who lived with his wife Cynthia in a maisonette in Finchley Road, Golders Green, London. It was discovered that his association with Setty took the form of a partnership in which Setty stole the cars and Hume sold them after they had been 'dealt with' as they termed it in those circles. Several other associates of Setty told police that it was quite possible that Hume could be involved in the missing man's disappearance because they understood that the £1,000 car deal, which appeared to be common knowledge among them, had been clinched between Setty and Hume.

The police now launched into an investigation of Hume's last known movements. It was quickly discovered that he had hired a light two-seater Auster aircraft from the United Service Flying Club at Elstree, of which he was a member holding a 'C' flying licence. It was remembered there that Hume had not paid for the hire of the aircraft on a previous occasion and that he had been told he could not take it out again until he had paid the bill for the previous trip. It was observed that Hume took out a thick wad of banknotes and peeled off the ten £5 bills required to settle the outstanding account, whereupon he was allowed to take the aeroplane out. It was noted at this time that he had with him two large parcels wrapped in some kind of greyish material and tied with cord. The date was 5 October – the day after Stanley Setty had disappeared.

The following day the personnel at the Elstree club had again hired out the same aircraft to Hume, who had paid the hire fee without ado, again from a large bankroll. This time, officials said, he had one parcel with him, similarly bundled. It was, of course, no business of the Club to know what these parcels contained, provided that they did not contravene flying regulations against the transportation of explosives or inflammable materials. A rather unusual feature of both these two trips was that on each occasion Hume had landed at places other than the Club's landing-grounds – he had landed at Southend and Gravesend respectively – and had then telephoned the Club to inform them of the whereabouts of the aircraft so that someone could come and collect it, saying that bad weather had forced him to land in an unscheduled place and, as he put it, 'abandon ship' because he had to get back to London on business. This point did not go unobserved, especially as it had happened on two occasions on two consecutive days. The weather at the time of the flights certainly left much to be desired, but the real reason was undoubtedly a matter of Hume's not wanting the Club to know that he had gone out with the bundles but had returned without them. The Club did not consider the matter suspicious in any way but thought it rather odd that a pilot of Hume's experience should have been unable to navigate correctly.

The police kept Hume under discreet surveillance; they had no proof at this stage that he was concerned in the disappearance of Setty, even if his behaviour in regard to the hire of the aircraft had been decidedly odd. There was no law to say that a private pilot could not take parcels with him on his aircraft, nor at that stage did they connect the existence of three parcels with the disappearance of the 'hot' car trader. But a few days later, on 21 October, the finding of Setty's torso in the Essex marshes would throw an entirely different light on the matter. The police put two and two together ...

It was time to take Brian Donald Hume in for questioning. He was apprehended at his home in Golders Green and taken to Albany Street Police Station. At first he said that he knew no one named Stanley Setty. He readily admitted that he had hired a two-seater Auster aircraft from the United Service Flying Club at Elstree, of which he was a member. He also admitted that he had thrown three parcels into the sea from the aircraft, two on the first trip and one on the second.

Asked what the parcels contained, Hume replied that they had contained parts of an illegal printing press used for forging petrol coupons (petrol was still rationed at that time) which had been handed to him by three men, known to him only by their nicknames of 'Mac', 'Greeny' and 'The Boy', who told him to dispose of them in such a way that they would never be found. In return for this service he would be paid a substantial sum of money. In case he demurred, Hume continued, one of the three men was 'toying with a gun' as he spoke. The three men had brought the three parcels to his flat while his wife was out. He did not know where they lived, and his vague descriptions of the men could have applied to half the men in London. Hume said that the police would be able to find all of them dealing in cars at the Warren Street kerbside, or in the pubs in the immediate vicinity. The police were sceptical about this story and did not believe the three men existed, but they went through the motions of looking for them, Hume remaining meanwhile in custody.

On 26 November Hume was sent for trial at Bow Street Magistrates' Court, charged with the murder of Stanley Setty. Hume pleaded not guilty at this preliminary hearing. The trial itself took place on 18 January 1950 at the Old Bailey before Mr Justice Lewis, who was replaced later by Mr Justice Sellers, due to sudden illness. Mr Christmas Humphreys prosecuted, and Mr R.F. Levy, KC, defended the accused.

Witnesses for the prosecution followed each other into the witness-box. First of all Mrs Stride, Hume's daily cleaning lady, gave evidence of how she had been requested by Hume to go out and buy another floor cloth as the one he had was spoilt owing to his having rubbed it on a stained carpet. She said that she did not attach any unusual significance to this request. Questioned further, she testified that she had neither heard nor seen anything unusual at the house on that day.

Next, Mrs Linda Hearnden, the manageress of a North London dry cleaners', told the Court how Hume had brought into her shop a badly stained light green carpet, asking her to have it dyed a deep shade of green. The next witness was an accountant from a North London branch of the Midland Bank, who stated that Hume, who had an overdraft of £78 at the time, came in on 6 October and paid in the sum of £90, thus clearing his overdraft and putting himself in credit.

Another witness was a mechanic at a garage in Golders Green who knew Hume. He said that on 5 October Hume had come in at about lunch-time and asked him to sharpen a large carving-knife. He had told Hume that his work was really with cars and that Hume should take it to a knife-grinder, but Hume replied that this man's shop was too far to go as he needed it for a lunch-time joint which was cooking. The mechanic sharpened it.

Mr Joseph Staddon, an interior decorator, related how on 6 October he had been called to Hume's maisonette to do some painting, which consisted mainly of re-staining the wood skirting-boards in the lounge. Asked why he wanted the job doing, Hume had replied that he had it done two or three times a year. Mr Staddon said that he considered this rather odd. He then went on to describe how, after he had completed the job, Hume had asked him to help him move a heavy package down the stairs and into his (Hume's) car. 'It was so heavy,' Mr Staddon testified, 'that it slid and bumped down the stairs, and it made some peculiar noises.'

He had asked Hume what was in the package, 'This is heavy, Guv! What have you got in it?'

Hume told him that he was transporting a consignment of fish.

Mr Staddon testified that the parcel was about 2 ft. 6 in. long and exceedingly heavy. 'I could not have lifted it by myself,' he said. This was hardly surprising, since Setty had been a very heavily built man.

William Davy, an aircraft fitter from the Elstree-based United Service Flying Club, testified that Hume, who was a member of the Club, had hired an Auster two-seater on 5 October and had taken the machine out carrying two parcels which he had brought with him. The aircraft had later been recovered from Southend, where Hume had left it, having reported landing difficulties owing to bad weather combined with navigation problems. Davy's testimony concluded with the statement that when he examined the aircraft on its return to base, there were quite definitely no parcels or bundles in it.

Various police officers then gave evidence that they had unsuccessfully searched the Warren Street area of London for three men who had been described by Hume as 'spivs' and who went under the sobriquets of 'Mac', 'Greeny' and 'The Boy'. In his own evidence, Hume persisted in this story of the three men, but the Court did not for one moment believe him, any more than the police had done. Hume had stated that the men had paid him £50 to dump the first two parcels and a further £50 to dispose of the third, and he continued to insist that they contained parts of an illicit press for printing counterfeit petrol coupons.

The evidence for the prosecution, Mr Humphreys said, was purely circumstantial. The proof that Hume had taken the parcels out in an aircraft and had returned without them was not proof of murder, even though the flights had been made on the two days following Setty's disappearance. But, the judge pointed out, Hume's movements on 4 October, the day Setty was presumed to have been killed, were not known. No one had seen any three men bringing any parcels to his flat – 'between 2 and 3 p.m., in broad daylight' – as the accused had stated in his evidence. 'Although the three parcels could well have contained Setty's dismembered remains,' the judge continued, 'there is no proof at any point in the prosecution's evidence that they did in fact contain them.'

More relevant was the fact that several banknotes had surfaced which were proved to have come from a sum of £1,000 in consecutively numbered banknotes which Setty had received on 4 October as his share of a deal involving stolen Wolseley cars. These were discovered in the money paid for the hire of the aircraft, the money paid into the Midland Bank to clear Hume's overdraft, and one £5 banknote given to a taxi-driver who took Hume in his cab from Southend to his Golders Green home, who had been traced. This, the judge pointed out, was still not proof of murder, even though it could be construed as proof that Setty had been robbed of this money and that the man who had robbed him could have been Hume.

The jury were unable to agree on a verdict, since the

evidence was insufficient to convict the accused of murder. They were discharged, and another jury sworn in, but the prosecution offered no further evidence and Hume was found not guilty of murder. A second indictment charging Hume with being an accessory to murder by disposing of a body was heard and, after a brief adjournment for consultation with the judge on a legal point, Hume pleaded guilty to this second charge and was sentenced to twelve years' imprisonment.

Prison, however, had not changed Hume's criminal propensities. On his release from Dartmoor on 1 February 1958, he launched himself into his new career of bank robber. But first he decided to cash in on his acquittal of murder and gain some recompense for the years he had spent in prison. He changed his name by deed poll to Donald Brown, booked into a smart hotel in Westcliff-on-Sea, and wrote a series of articles under the title 'Confessions', which he sold to the *Sunday Pictorial*, who serialized them. Hume, knowing that he could not be tried again for a murder of which he had been acquitted, let rip in these articles with a full and detailed account of how he had killed Stanley Setty during the course of a quarrel, and admitting that 'Mac', 'Greeny' and 'The Boy' were a figment of his imagination intended to fox the police.

On the night of 4 October 1949, his 'Confessions' stated, he returned from a drinking session to find Setty in his flat. His wife and baby had gone to visit her mother. It was not made clear in the article whether his wife had let him in in order that he might wait for her husband to come home, or whether he, as his business associate, had his own key. Be that as it may, a quarrel developed between them, and Hume – in self-defence, he said – seized a German dagger hanging on the wall, which was part of a collection of Second World War souvenirs. 'I was wielding the dagger,' he wrote, 'just as our Stone Age ancestors did 20,000 years ago.' What he seemed to have forgotten was the fact that our Stone Age ancestors wielded stone weapons, not German daggers from the Second World War. He went on to describe how he 'watched Setty's life run from him like water down a drain'. Setty died from multiple stab wounds to the chest and stomach.

Hume realized that his wife and baby could return at any time, so he bundled Setty's body into the coal-hole, cleaned up the blood and rearranged the rugs to cover stains on the carpet, and changed his own clothes. He then took Setty's car keys from his pocket and drove his Citroën car, which was parked outside, to Regent's Park leaving it outside the house where Setty lived, with the keys in the ignition after wiping them and the car clean of any fingerprints he might have made. He then returned home and meticulously wiped all fingerprints from his flat – so efficiently, indeed, that the police were unable to find a single print when they searched the flat.

On the following morning his wife had a hospital appointment for a check-up, and Hume calculated that he would have just under an hour and a half to dismember the body, so he would be working against the clock. First he went just round the corner and purchased a hack-saw, then went to the garage nearby where he had a carving-knife sharpened. He was surprised to find that it was not as difficult as he had feared it would be to cut off the head and legs from the corpse, but, he said, it was strange that no one heard him as he was performing this task, as 'sawing bones is very noisy work' and, since his knowledge of anatomy was not very good, he made himself more work than he need have done otherwise by sawing through the actual bones instead of through the ligaments and joints that held them together.

He then bundled up the three portions of the body into felt-wrapped parcels tied securely with cord. He put the torso back in the coal-hole and took the other parts downstairs and into his car. It was not made clear in his account what he did with Setty's clothing, but he said that he removed his wallet containing the £1,000 bankroll plus his other money, and claimed that most of this money was so badly bloodstained that he had to burn it. Anyone who would believe that would believe anything!

Hume wasted no time but left for Elstree immediately, and the rest of the story we know from his account given in his evidence at the Old Bailey, except that in his published 'Confessions' he adds that he also jettisoned the German dagger, the knife and the hack-saw at the same time that he dropped the bundles into the sea. He did not say whether his wife had noticed the unexplained absence of the dagger from the collection, or the carving-knife from her kitchen, but doubtless with his facility for concocting cock-and-bull stories, he was able to fabricate some plausible excuse to convince her.

Hume, soon after the publication of his 'Confessions', embarked on armed bank robbery for a living, after first enjoying a holiday in Europe, where he spent a good deal of the £2,000 he had been paid by the *Sunday Pictorial*. At 12 noon on 2 August 1958 he entered the Midland Bank branch in Boston Manor Road, Brentford, Middlesex, brandishing a revolver with which he shot and wounded a cashier, Mr Frank Lewis, and escaped with £1,500. The same day he flew to Zürich, where he lay low and attempted to disguise his appearance by changing his hairstyle, growing a moustache and donning spectacles. On 12 November he was back in London again, and soon afterwards had the temerity to rob the same bank again. This time he shot the manager, though not fatally, and escaped with only £300, running out of the building and catching a train at Kew Bridge to take him to Waterloo, where he put on his spectacles, arranged a wig over his hair, and left his raincoat in the toilet. That same evening he was back in Zürich.

His dumping of the raincoat was a serious mistake.

Inside was a name-tape bearing one of Hume's known aliases, and the Brentford bank staff's description of the raider convinced the police that it was Hume they should be seeking. But Hume had eluded them once again ...

Hume, back in Zürich, had other ideas. On 30 January 1959, Hume, now calling himself John Bird, visited the Gewerbe Bank, but not as a customer. He was armed with a sawn-off shotgun concealed in a cardboard box. He shot and wounded a cashier, but all he got for his pains were a few bags of loose coins. The alarm bell sounded, and he ran, hotly pursued by bank staff and passers-by. A 50-year-old taxi-driver threatened his escape by trying to block his path with his cab; he was shot dead. Police swarmed into the area and captured the raider.

A Swiss psychiatrist, Dr Guggenheim, examined Hume in prison and pronounced him sane – in other words, he knew what he was doing. He was brought to trial in Zürich on the charge of murdering Arthur Maag, the taxi-driver, and was sentenced to life imprisonment on being found guilty by a unanimous verdict. Held in solitary confinement in Regensdorf Jail, he kept fit by means of physical exercise programmes, and kept his mind occupied by writing a novel, entitled *The Dead Stay Dumb*, about gangsters and their exploits, with which he obviously identified himself. A Catholic priest who visited him voiced the opinion that he was a psychopath.

In August 1976, his behaviour in prison having deteriorated to an alarming extent, his case was brought before a Swiss court, and doctors pronouncing him insane, the authorities decided to return him to Britain, where he was sent to Broadmoor in August 1976.

2

The Brighton Trunk Murders

Unsolved (1934)

Truth is stranger than fiction. What crime fiction writer would have a body turn up in a trunk in a railway station left-luggage office, on Derby Day of all times, and then have a second body turn up in another trunk in the very same town only a week later? And as if that were not enough, have the police, while conducting a house-to-house search in connection with the first murder, routinely interview a man who at that precise time had the body of the second victim in a trunk in his flat? It would be too far-fetched to ring true. Yet that is precisely what happened, in 1934.

Brighton, on Derby Day that year, was full of holidaymakers and day-trippers, enjoying the brilliant sunshine. Ice-cream vendors were doing a roaring trade, and the beach was packed with sunbathers and swimmers with their colourful towels, deck chairs and picnic baskets. But there were one or two folks who were not quite so carefree – in fact, they were quite concerned. They were the luggage deposit office clerks who were responsible for the suitcases, trunks and other travel gear left by various railway passengers. A foul stench was gradually pervading the office with its rows of shelves. At first the clerks thought it must be a dead animal – perhaps a cat – which had somehow got into the building and found its way into some secluded corner of the office to die. As the odour grew stronger by the day, they searched the office, including the cupboards and cubby-holes, but could find no trace of anything untoward. Finally, they decided that the stench must be coming from one of the items of left luggage on the shelves. A sniffing session along these shelves soon discovered the culprit – a large black trunk with a rounded top, known as a steamer trunk from the fact that it was of the type frequently used on board ship. The clerks were not allowed to open passengers' luggage, so they decided to call the police.

The police, of course, had no such qualms about opening the trunk, which they forced with a crowbar. As the lid sprang open, the nude torso of a female was revealed to their astonished gaze. The trunk with its grisly contents was hauled off to the mortuary to be examined by forensic experts, who pronounced it to be the body of a woman of about thirty, who had been about five months pregnant.

It seemed to the police investigating the murder that the person who had left the trunk containing the torso at Brighton might well have travelled either to or from Brighton on a London train in order to deposit another piece of luggage containing another part, or parts, of the same body in another railway station luggage office. In this speculation they proved to be right on target, for an intensive search of left-luggage offices in all the London main line stations produced a suitcase at King's Cross, which contained the legs which forensic pathologists soon determined had come from the same body. All that could be ascertained from these legs was that the feet had been meticulously cared for, most probably by a chiropodist with a professional pedicure. Thus, it was assumed that the dead woman was of what was termed the 'middle class' type of background.

The search continued for the missing arms and the head, which were never found. It is most likely that the killer of this woman took great pains to dispose of them in such a way as to ensure that they would never come to light. It is almost impossible to identify a body and legs without the head, and without the hands from which fingerprints can be taken. The murder was never solved, and the unfortunate victim's identity is unknown to this day.

During the course of routine house-to-house inquiries, the police visited hundreds of houses and flats in the general vicinity of Brighton railway station, on the premise that the person who had killed the trunk victim would in all probability have lived fairly near to such a convenient place to dump a body, or part of a body. Among the addresses they visited was a basement flat at 52 Kemp Street. The tenant of this flat was a man named Tony Mancini, a man of several aliases and whose real name was Cecil Louis England, but who was known as Tony Mancini at the material time and had been using this name for some considerable time. He was a 26-year-old petty crook who had come to Brighton from London and had taken a job as a waiter in a café called the Skylark Café. Prior to taking this job he had been living on the earnings of his mistress, who was a prostitute. He gave the police a satisfactory account of his whereabouts at the presumed time of death of the trunk victim.

The railway staff could not remember any particular man who had deposited the trunk in the left-luggage office, since on Derby Day the town was thronged with visitors and several dozen people had deposited luggage. It was therefore impossible to obtain from these clerks a description which could be compared with the persons interviewed during the house-to-house inquiries.

After a full week of these interviews, the police were still no nearer to solving the case, and the Brighton trunk murderer remained as elusive as ever. They decided that a search of the premises they had visited was in order, hoping that such a course of action would reveal some small clue to the identity of the murderer, or even the victim's missing head and arms hidden in some out-of-the-way place such as a coal-hole or a garden shed. They fervently hoped that they would not have to dig up gardens; it would be difficult enough conducting house searches. They relied on the fact that the vast majority of householders, as anxious as the police to see the killer apprehended, would give them permission voluntarily. Search warrants required a court order and the police were loth to enter into negotiations of such a nature if it could possibly be avoided.

All the householders previously interviewed were quite willing to have a couple of officers look round their homes without disturbing anything unless they had good and sufficient reason, and they encountered no problems until they called once again at the basement flat at 52 Kemp Street. No one was at home on this occasion. In accordance with their normal procedure, they made inquiries of the residents of adjoining properties and the tenants on the floors above the basement flat. They were told that Tony Mancini had left a few days before. None of them had any idea where he had gone, but one neighbour volunteered the information that she thought he had moved back to London where he had originally come from.

The landlady, who had the flat on the ground floor immediately above the basement flat, was much more forthcoming. She told the police that Mancini had taken the flat a few days before they had been calling at the houses to make their door-to-door inquiries, bringing with him some luggage which included a large black cabin trunk. This trunk, she said, was extremely heavy and she had to call two of the other lodgers to help get it down the stairs. When she asked him what it contained, he said it was books. She pointed out that some kind of dark fluid was oozing from the bottom and told him to wipe this up so that it would not stain the lino or rugs. He told her that it was a bottle of French polish he had been using to refinish some chairs.

Asked if Mancini had taken the trunk with him when he moved out, she said that she did not know. She had not actually seen him go; he had just come and paid her the rent he owed the day before leaving. He had not told her of his intention to leave. A few days afterwards some of her other tenants began complaining of a foul odour which seemed to emanate from the basement flat, which she had not yet had time to get ready for re-letting. She said she had not gone into the flat to investigate where the smell was coming from because she had temporarily mislaid her key and Mancini had omitted to return his key when he left. She had noticed the smell herself one day when passing the basement flat door on her way to the area to put rubbish in the dustbin, and thought that she ought to ring the council, but had not yet had time to do so.

The two police officers were pretty sure what the smell was coming from. The missing head and arms of the murder victim, together with Mancini's precipitate disappearance without benefit of telling his landlady that he was leaving, pointed to a solution to the mystery. They forced the door to the basement flat, since the landlady still could not find where she had put her key.

In one of the rooms was a black cabin trunk very similar to the one which had been left at Brighton Station left luggage office. And the seepage from the bottom of the trunk, which the landlady had noticed when Mancini had brought it into the house, was now much more than just a trickle. The landlady's sharp intake of breath as she saw it was probably at least partly due to the sight of the stained floorboards as to the stench which overwhelmed the three of them as they entered the room. An officer gingerly tried to raise the lid. It would not budge. Unlike the officers who had prised open the lid of the railway trunk with a crowbar, these two had nothing with them which would do the job. They asked the landlady if she had anything, and she went and fetched a chopper from the coal-hole. The officer was able to lever up the lid by sliding the blade underneath at what looked like its weakest point – the trunk was obviously an old and much-used one.

Imagine their astonishment when the opened lid revealed to their horrified gaze not a human head or arms, but a *whole female body*!

The body was nude, and had been doubled up in order to cram it into the trunk. Decomposition was in a fairly advanced stage. The police were incredulous. It was only one week after the discovery of the railway torso – the date was 14 July – and already they had two murdered women stuffed into almost identical black steamer trunks in the same town. It seemed they had a multiple trunk murderer loose in their midst – even if he had disappeared. Mancini was the obvious suspect. But who were the two women?

Forensic examination pronounced the body from the Kemp Street flat to be that of a woman between thirty-five and forty years of age. Death had been caused by a violent blow from a blunt instrument such as a hammer, which had caused a depressed fracture of the skull. Unlike the first victim, this one had not been pregnant. She had been about 5 ft. 7 in. in height, with long dark hair and blue eyes, and of medium build. The killer must have had quite a job getting her to fit into the trunk. The autopsy report stated that she had been dead for about six weeks.

Speculation was rife, even among the police. If, indeed, the two women had been murdered by the same man, then the second body must have been the first victim, since the railway torso had been found to be in a much fresher condition, probably dead only a few days. However, there was no proof whatsoever that both victims had been killed by the same person. In fact, several officers voiced the opinion that a man who could easily dispose of a dismembered body by leaving parts in various left luggage offices in places as far apart as Brighton and London, would scarcely leave another victim whole, put her into a trunk and then leave the trunk in his lodgings while he left the area. Although it was not unknown for multiple killers to change their MO (*modus operandi* or method of operation), it was not usual. 'Tried and tested' methods of disposal seemed to be the general rule. So one theory was that there were *two* trunk murderers in Brighton – a sobering thought but one which made local newspaper circulations soar sky-high. The sensation also brought the morbid flocking to Brighton in greater numbers than the Derby Day crowds. The Brighton Trunk Murders also, of course, made national headlines in the tabloids.

Meanwhile, where was Mancini? Inquiries revealed several interesting points. He had moved to the Kemp Street address from a flat at 44 Park Crescent, not far from Kemp Street. At the Park Crescent flat he had been living with a woman, and they were known to the landlord as 'Mr and Mrs Watson'. The woman's real name was Violette Kaye, thirty-eight years of age, who was a prostitute. Mancini had no job at that time and lived on her earnings.

About six weeks before moving to Kemp Street, Mrs Olive Watts, Violette Kaye's sister, who lived in London and had been intending to visit her for a few days, received a telegram as follows:

=GOING ABROAD STOP GOOD JOB STOP SAIL SUNDAY STOP
WILL WRITE STOP=

=VI=

The telegram was hand-written, but was not in Violette Kaye's hand. It was later proved to have been written by Mancini.

At about the same time Mancini was putting it about that his mistress had left him and had gone to Paris to take up a job. When asked what kind of job, he told friends and neighbours that she was going to work as a dancer in a nightclub.

Detectives now searched the premises at 44 Park Crescent, which had remained unoccupied since Mancini had moved. A charred hammer was found in the fireplace, but there were no bloodstains or other evidence to be revealed. The dead woman's clothing, too, was missing. In fact the only evidence of previous occupation left in the flat were a few cooking-pots, crockery and other kitchen utensils.

A description of Mancini was circulated and he was soon located – on 17 July – by a Kentish policeman on routine patrol duties some way out of Maidstone, in the early hours. He seemed to have been wandering about in a dazed condition. When apprehended, he readily admitted his identity.

'Yes, I am the man you are looking for,' he told the constable. 'I am Tony Mancini.'

'We want to ask you some questions about the death in Brighton of a woman named Violette Kaye,' the officer said.

'Yes, I knew Violette Kaye. But I did not kill her,' Mancini replied.

Mancini was taken back to Brighton police station where he was interrogated at length by Chief Inspector James Donaldson. He had been put in charge of the investigation into both the trunk murders by the Sussex County Constabulary. Eventually, Mancini was charged with the murder of Violette Kaye. They had no evidence to connect him with the railway trunk murder. 'All I can say is that I am not guilty,' the prisoner said. 'I never killed her.'

All he would admit to was that Violette Kaye, who had been his mistress, was a prostitute and that she entertained clients at their flat with his knowledge and consent. His story was that on 10 May he had returned to the flat after taking a walk while she was thus occupied, and on his return he had found her lying dead on the bed. He stated that there was a stocking tied round her neck and that there was blood on the sheets. He assumed that the last client she had been with had killed her, for some unknown reason, possibly during a dispute over money which got out of hand.

When asked why he had not reported his find to the police, Mancini said:

> I was too scared. I would never be able to convince the police that it was not me. I knew they would blame me because I have a criminal record. I couldn't prove I didn't kill her, so I went out and went for a walk along the beach trying to think out what to do ... I hadn't the courage to go to the police and tell them what I had found. I decided that the best thing would be to move, and take the body with me and keep it until I had decided how best to dispose of it. I don't know who killed her. There were so many men coming to the flat, it could have been any one of them. I rarely ever saw any of them as I always had to go out before they turned up.

When told that the autopsy report made no mention of the use of a stocking or any other ligature around the neck of the deceased, Mancini insisted that he had seen a stocking so placed. He was told that the autopsy had shown that she had been killed by a violent blow to the head, and had not been strangled. He replied, 'OK, so she wasn't strangled, but there was definitely a stocking round her neck.'

At his committal hearing, Brighton magistrates sent him for trial at the Sussex Assizes in Lewes on 10 December 1934, pending which time he remained in prison. By this time the police, after conducting a good many interviews with him, were as certain as they could be that Mancini had no link with the railway trunk murder. The search for the perpetrator of the latter crime continued unabated, but no leads were forthcoming, and after a length of time, it was quietly dropped and they concentrated on Mancini as the prime suspect in the murder of Violette Kaye.

One of the foremost advocates of the day, Norman Birkett KC, agreed to defend Mancini. Although he knew that the suspect had a lengthy prison record, this was for petty larceny, theft, fraud and similar crimes, with no history of violence. A man could be a worthless scoundrel, supporting himself on the proceeds of crime and living on immoral earnings, but that did not make him a murderer. Such was Birkett's reasoning.

The trial opened on the scheduled date of 10 December before Mr Justice Branson. Birkett's juniors were Mr John Flowers KC and Mr Eric Neve. The prosecution was led by Mr J.D. Cassels KC (later Mr Justice Cassels), accompanied by Mr Quintin Hogg (later Lord Hailsham, Lord Chancellor).

As Mancini was led into the court, he was booed, hissed and cat-called by milling crowds outside who hurled abuse as well as eggs and tomatoes. When asked how he pled, he replied, 'I am not guilty.' The Crown then called a number of witnesses for the prosecution. One of these was Henry Snuggs, the landlord of the premises at 44 Park Crescent where Mancini had shared a flat with the unfortunate Violette Kaye.

Snuggs testified that he had let a flat in his house to the accused and a woman, whom he knew as 'Mr and Mrs Watson'. He related that he had not observed anything unusual about the couple, apart from one incident when, during the second week of May, about two months after they had taken the tenancy of the flat, he heard Mancini running up and down the stairs at a fast speed, as though in a great rush, very late at night. The sound had awakened him. Later, Snuggs testified, on 14 May he saw Mancini in the hall with a young woman he did not know, whom Mancini introduced as his sister, Miss Geraldine Watson. On this particular occasion Mancini told him that he would be leaving shortly, as his wife had deserted him and gone to France to take up an offer of employment as a dancer in a nightclub.

Asked by Birkett in cross-examination whether he had ever seen or heard the couple quarrelling, Snuggs answered emphatically in the negative. 'They seemed always on the most affectionate of terms,' he averred.

Several more witnesses were now examined and cross-examined including tenants of other flats at 44 Park Crescent who described the large number of male visitors, and a Brighton market stallholder who testified that Mancini had purchased from him a second-hand black leather cabin trunk, for which he paid 7s. 6d.

Violette Kaye was known to have been alive on 10 May, since a witness, Thomas Kerslake, testified that he had seen her on that date standing in the doorway of 44 Park Crescent and had a brief conversation with her. Kerslake was probably the last person to have seen Violette Kaye alive.

The next witness to be called was Mrs Alice Watts, the sister of the dead woman, who testified that a telegram she had received, purporting to be from her sister cancelling their pre-arranged holiday, stated that she was going abroad to take up a job. The handwriting was definitely not that of her sister. A graphologist was called to give evidence that the handwriting on this telegram was identical to that on a menu written out for the Skylark Café in Brighton, at which Mancini had briefly taken a job as a waiter. One of Mancini's duties while there was to write out the menu cards each day.

Joyce Golding, a waitress employed at the Skylark Café, told the court of a noisy quarrel which had taken place between Mancini and Violette Kaye, who had come to the café in a very bad temper. On the following day, Mancini had taken her (Miss Golding) to a dance in the town, and invited her home with him, to which she had agreed. While there he gave her a number of items of female clothing, saying they had belonged to Violette Kaye, who had left him and gone to France.

The next witness to be called was Dr Roche Lynch, the Home Office analyst. He testified that his examination of Mancini's clothing, including two shirts and two pairs of trousers, had revealed bloodstains, but that he had been unable to ascertain the blood group of these stains, nor had he been able to ascertain the blood group of the deceased, owing to the advanced state of decomposition of the body. Dr Lynch had also examined the charred hammer which had been found in the fireplace at 44 Park Crescent, but stated that if indeed this object had at one time borne bloodstains, these would have been completely obliterated by the burning.

Cross-examined by Norman Birkett, when Dr Lynch pointed out that the blood on one of the shirts appeared to have been splashed on to it from another source rather than having emanated from a cut suffered by the person wearing the shirt, Birkett said that he would be able to prove that the shirt was not purchased by Mancini until after the death of Violette Kaye. The advocate likewise told the court that he would be able to prove that at least one of the pairs of bloodstained trousers could not have been worn by the accused until after the woman's death, because they had been only on order at the time. Birkett called the tailor concerned, who stated that the trousers were not delivered until June.

After the examination and cross-examination of a number of minor witnesses, all of whom had some small but not insignificant contribution to make to the evidence either for or against the accused, Tony Mancini himself was called to the stand. After some preliminary questioning about his life with the deceased, he was asked to give an account of her last day. She had come to see him in the Skylark Café where he was working as a waiter, Mancini told the court, and appeared to be considerably the worse for drink. She was in 'a filthy temper' and launched into a tirade against him. He said that he simply ignored her outburst – 'it was only the drink talking' – and eventually she flounced out, still shouting abuse. The owner of the café called him and told him that he could not afford to risk losing customers by having this kind of behaviour in his establishment, and warned him that it must cease.

When Mancini returned home that evening, he continued, he found the front door to his flat wide open, which was very unusual as it was normally kept locked. He said that he felt somewhat apprehensive as he entered. He could see no sign of Violette Kaye until he went into the bedroom, where he observed her coat lying on the floor. This, too, was unusual, he said, as she was always tidy and hung up her clothes after taking them off. Then he saw that she was lying on the bed 'in a peculiar position'. Asked to describe what he meant by this, he said:

She was sort of hunched up and clutching sheets in her hand. Then I saw a stocking round her neck and blood on the sheets. I felt her pulse, but there was no response. I felt her heart, but it was not beating. It was then I realized that she was dead. I was stunned. I just did not know what to do.

Asked how he thought she had died, he replied, 'One of her clients must have killed her during an argument.' He then described how he had panicked and gone out for a walk to think out what he should do. His explanation of why he did not go to the police was substantially the same as that he had given to the detectives who had interrogated him at Brighton police station.

Under cross-examination by Cassels, Mancini stuck doggedly to the same story. Cassels was scathing. He told Mancini point-blank that his version of events was a cock-and-bull story he had fabricated to divert suspicion from himself, and that it was the Crown's contention that he had killed Violette Kaye with a blow on the head from the hammer which had subsequently been found in the fireplace at 44 Park Crescent. To all this Mancini listened attentively, and then turned to the judge and said simply, 'I did not kill her, my lord.'

Cassels pointed out that the hammer which the Crown contended was the murder weapon had been charred by being burnt in the fireplace to destroy the bloodstains. On further cross-examination, Birkett said that the hammer could quite easily have been scooped up with the coal and inadvertently burnt when making the fire. But he was also at pains to point out that this explanation, although feasible, was not very likely. People did not usually tip such large quantities of coal on to a fire that a hammer buried in it would go unnoticed, but if it did, it could easily have been raked out later with the ashes. However, Birkett voiced the opinion that a murderer who had committed such a foul deed would be much more likely to have gone out to dispose of it elsewhere in such a way as to ensure that it would never be found. One way would have been to walk to the end of the pier and drop it unobserved into the sea; another way would have been to hire a pleasure boat and row out as far as he could from shore to achieve the same end.

Norman Birkett's speech, which took over an hour, was enough to sow the seeds of doubt in the minds of any jury. 'I demand of you a verdict of Not Guilty!' Everyone in court thought that at this point he had concluded his speech. There was a dramatic and pregnant pause. Then his last words came: 'Stand firm!'

The prosecutor's final speech was short, succinct and to the point. It took the form of knocking as many holes as possible in Birkett's arguments.

> A man who was innocent of this crime would hardly be likely to move from one lodging to another, taking with him the body of his victim in a trunk, and keeping it in his new lodging for six weeks, before finally fleeing the town, leaving the trunk containing the by now rapidly decomposing corpse behind. Does that make sense to you as the action of an innocent man? I call upon you, the jury, to use your brains and not your emotions to guide you in arriving at your considered verdict of guilty of murder.

The judge's summing-up was fair and impartial. He uttered a word of warning to the jurors: 'This is not a court of morals but a court of law, and you must not allow the natural revulsion which one must feel against a man who lives in this manner to affect your judgment against him. He is not on trial for his mode of life but for the murder of a fellow human being.'

The jury was out for two-and-a-half hours before returning a unanimous verdict of Not Guilty. At this pronouncement, Mancini appeared dazed, as though stunned by the verdict – one which he had not expected. He could scarcely believe that he was free to go. 'Not guilty, Mr. Birkett?' he asked. 'Did I hear it correctly? Not guilty, Mr. Birkett?' His counsel assured him that it was adjudged so.

With the acquittal of Tony Mancini, the second Brighton trunk murder was officially pronounced unsolved. But it is significant that the police made no further efforts to trace the supposed killer of Violette Kaye …

*   *   *

Forty years later, Tony Mancini made headlines in the *News of the World* with his confession to journalist Alan Hart that he had indeed murdered Violette Kaye in 1934. The article, which appeared in the *News of the World* dated 28 November 1976 headlined I GOT AWAY WITH MURDER, had been preceded by a series detailing his past life on the fringes of the underworld, including his involvement with gangland figures and other sordid episodes. Mancini, now seventy years of age, could not be tried again for the murder. One puzzle raised during the trial was seemingly solved in his confession. He stated that he had not hit his mistress with the hammer but that he had banged her head on the brass fender and that it was this that had fractured her skull and caused her death. He said that the hammer was kept in the coal scuttle to break large lumps of coal, and that after he had come back from his long walk on the beach (and a visit to several pubs on the way home) he sat up in a chair all night and, feeling cold, had lit the fire and must have dropped the hammer into the fire while breaking up coals in a drunken state.

The pathologist who had performed the autopsy on Violette Kaye was none other than the great Spilsbury. If he had lived to read Mancini's confession, he would have been fuming at having his evidence as to the cause of the blow so discredited. Spilsbury was well known to be a man who could not bear to be proved wrong.

3

The Tale of a Duck

Frederick Thorne (1897)

You know the old saying: if it looks like a duck, waddles like a duck and quacks like a duck – ten to one it's a duck! A smallholder who had a tiny farm in a rural area of the New York suburb of Woodstock had a pond behind the farmhouse, and on this pond he kept a white duck. It was more of a family pet than anything, for it was several years old and never laid any eggs.

Ted Lancing, the homesteader, was out one day in the kitchen garden behind his house, attending to some of the plots which needed hoeing to get rid of the weeds. He paused to take a rest and looked up, and the sight that met his gaze stopped him dead in his tracks. He couldn't believe his eyes. There was his duck – at least it was the same size as his bird and was making its way purposefully to its pond. But it was not a white duck. It was *pink*!

Ted rubbed his eyes in bewilderment. It seemed like his own bird – it had the same gait, it was the same size, and it obviously knew its own pond. But who ever heard of a *pink* duck? The birds come in many colours, but pink was

41

not one of them. Ted decided that this strange phenomenon needed looking into.

Ted knew that his pet liked to amble around the area after its morning feed, so the next day he followed the bird on its customary rambles. It led him to another small pond at the side of a house several hundred yards from his own property. The water was blood-red. In fact it looked more like blood than water, although it was a mixture of both. His duck had swum in this pond – as it now started to do again – and dyed its feathers blood-red in the process. After leaving the pond the colour had faded to a bright pink as its feathers dried in the air during its waddle home.

'Well, I'll be goddamned!' Ted cried out aloud. 'Something is not quite right here, that's for sure.' He pondered the problem for quite some time, and finally decided to go and see his friend and neighbour who was a sheriff's deputy. He would know what to do.

But let us now go back to the beginning. It all started in June 1897 in New York City, when two young teenage boys went for a swim in New York's river. A disused dock adjoining East 11th Street was a favourite location for the young lads of the neighbourhood. It was very early in the morning and the two, one thirteen and one fourteen, had the place to themselves.

They were enjoying their swim, splashing about and having great fun, when they spotted a brightly wrapped package floating in the water. Intrigued, they swam out and pushed it along until they reached the shore. The wrapping was of red oilcloth, decorated with a pattern of gold stars. Wondering what it could possibly be, they undid the cords that bound the parcel together, and there, revealed to their horrified gaze, was the upper torso of a male human body, complete with arms. Leaving their find on the bank, they precipitately threw on their clothes and hot-footed it to the nearest police station to report their find.

The following day another two boys had a similar nasty shock. These two were not swimming, but were busy gathering wild berries at an overgrown scrubland site on the Bronx side of the Harlem River, near the bottom of East 176th Street. Washed up on the bank, quite near the water's edge, they espied a similarly wrapped parcel.

These two boys, slightly older than the two swimmers, were equally intrigued, and on opening the parcel they found the lower part of a man's torso, from which the legs had been crudely severed.

It was not long before the legs turned up to complete the human jigsaw puzzle – complete, that is, except for the head. The legs were found by some sailors from the USS *Vermont*, at the US Naval Yard in Brooklyn. The legs, wrapped in similar fashion to the other parts, were bobbing on the surface of the water in the dock, four days after the first two finds.

Pathologists were able to confirm that all the parts belonged to the same body, and it was found that even the cut edges of the red oilcloth matched exactly. A small section of skin had been removed from the area below the left breast; it was thought that this was to remove an identifying mark such as a scar or a tattoo. The man's weight was estimated at 180 pounds (just under 13 stone), and the body was powerfully muscled, especially the arms and shoulders. A boxer, perhaps, or a wrestler? The man had been in tip-top physical condition. He was white, and his skin was not tanned, which seemed to point to his having had an indoor occupation.

The hands had their own story to tell. Carefully manicured and devoid of any calluses, they were certainly not the hands of a manual labourer. The man's occupation was an important point if it could be determined, since it might well provide a clue to his identity. Police, newspaper reporters and the public were all putting forward various theories based on the facts which had been put together in the autopsy room. Of course, if they only had the head, things would be a lot easier; it is very difficult indeed to identify a body without the head, unless the body has some distinguishing feature such as a scar, a tattoo, or an old fracture which shows up in an X-ray.

A very enthusiastic young medical student, still only in his first year of training, came up with an incredibly correct estimate, based simply on the known postulates. First of all, the student stated, the powerful arms and shoulders, combined with the well-kept and manicured nails and hands, pointed to a masseur, such as those employed in Turkish baths. Such a man, massaging upwards of two dozen men every day, would build a massive chest, shoulder and arm musculature, and his hands and nails would have to be soft and with no hard skin, rough patches or brittle nails to dig into a client's flesh. Working in a Turkish bath establishment was a full-time indoor job, so such a man would have little opportunity, if any, to acquire a tan.

He was proved to be absolutely correct when Lieutenant William Craddock, the police officer in charge of the investigation, visited the Turkish baths of New York – of which there were hundreds at that time, so fortunately for him he had not gone very far when at his fifth call he struck oil. The manager of this establishment told him that one of his masseurs, Willie Guldensuppe, had asked for the previous Friday off. This had been granted, on the understanding that he would report for work as usual the following morning. He never turned up, and had not been seen since. None of his fellow employees had any knowledge of what had happened to him. The manager was not unduly worried. 'They come and they go,' he said.

Willie Guldensuppe's description matched that of the dismembered corpse in the morgue. It was known that

Willie had a tattoo on his chest, in the same area as that from which the skin had been removed. Poor Willie had lost his head, but this did not stop him from being identified.

Obtaining Willie's address from the manager of the baths, investigators went there and found it to be occupied by a massive 16-stone woman, 5 ft. 6 in. tall, who went by the name of Augusta Nack. Yes, she told them, she certainly knew Willie Guldensuppe – after all, they had lived together for several years. But earlier this month he had left her and moved out, and she had no idea where he had gone. She now had a new live-in partner, one Frederick Thorne.

Willie, however, had continued to see his former mistress on occasions, and it would seem that Mrs Nack was not averse to the arrangement. Eventually, it transpired, Augusta herself wearied of the double life entailed by seeing Willie at times when Fred was at work. Fred, too, was becoming increasingly jealous. He was fully aware that Augusta was seeing Willie behind his back, and was not prepared to put up with it. They hatched a sinister plot: Augusta would invite Willie to the house, saying that Fred would be at work, when in reality Fred would be hiding in another room – with a gun.

Willie Guldensuppe fell for the ruse, and was shot in the head for his pains. The house stood in an isolated rural location and shots would not be heard by anybody. The murderous pair put the masseur's body into the bathtub and cut his throat with a razor to drain all the blood from the body. They then sawed it in half and cut off the head and the legs. The head they encased in plaster of Paris, and the rest of the body they parcelled up in pieces of red oilcloth and tied the bundles securely with cord. They then disposed of the grisly parcels by dropping them into the river under cover of darkness. The head never surfaced, weighted as it was with its plaster cast.

The next job the pair had to face was scrubbing out the bathtub with soap and water and bleach. In those days, one could not just turn the tap on – one had to bring in water from an outside pump and boil it on the stove, so it was a long job. At last they were satisfied that the bathtub was once more gleaming white. What they did not realize, however, was that the waste-pipe did not connect with any sewage system, but ran directly outside and emptied into the pond at the side of the house.

Augusta Nack and Frederick Thorne were arrested. In court, a shopkeeper testified that he had sold to Mrs Nack several yards of red oilcloth with a gold star pattern identical to the pieces exhibited in court as those that had been wrapped round the mortal remains of Willie Guldensuppe. Eventually, Mrs Nack was allowed to plead guilty to first-degree manslaughter in return for testifying against her lover Frederick Thorne. She was given a fifteen-year prison sentence for her complicity in the murder, but Fred was not so lucky. He went to the electric chair in Sing Sing in August 1898.

Murders have been solved by some bizarre clues in their time, but the clue of the duck that turned pink must surely be unique in the annals of crime.

4

Death of a Bag Lady

Robert Lee (1987)

Nobody knew much about her – the woman they called 'Sis' – not even her name. They did not know where she came from, whether she had any family, or even her exact age – she was thought to be about thirty years old. She helped out in a soup kitchen run by a church mission for the destitute and homeless. She had attended regularly for about three years, and was given food there every day. Sitting at one of the long refectory-style tables, she would eat in silence, never talking about herself. Occasionally she would make small-talk about the weather or some other neutral topic, but that was all. She was obviously very enthusiastic about her work at the mission, polishing the huge copper tea-urn, cutting huge mounds of bread, washing dishes, patching and mending the old clothes given to the tramps and dossers.

When Sis did not show for seven days on the trot, which was completely out of character for her, two of the regulars, who considered themselves to be the nearest thing to friends their mystery woman had, grew so concerned that they decided to do a bit of low-profile reconnoitring. They knew that Sis lived alone in a makeshift shelter she had built from old packing cases, crates, tin and sheet plastic on a derelict wooded lot not very far, as the crow flies, from the mission. They decided to go and see if they could find her there – perhaps she was ill and unable to get out. If they did not locate her, they would not be able to ask the neighbours, because there weren't any. The piece of woodland was quite isolated – which was why the reclusive Sis had chosen it for her home.

The two men, Bill Caldwell and Tony Chaffee, were homeless dossers who usually slept rough where they could – under bridges, in shop doorways and the like. The mission did not have overnight accommodation, but provided only food and second-hand clothing, and there were showers and toilets.

When Bill and Tony reached the shack, they immediately knew that something was very wrong. There was an overpowering stench which all but knocked them out, but it did not seem to emanate from the building itself, but rather from the small vegetable plot behind it. The two men looked at one another. They knew what they had to do …

So, on the morning of Sunday, 21 September 1986, Bill and Tony presented themselves at police headquarters in Bloomington, Indiana, to report their suspicions. Two officers were despatched to accompany the men to the wooded lot, and on seeing the makeshift shack they turned to their informants incredulously. 'Your friend lived here alone?' they said.

'She did,' Bill replied.

'How long for?' asked one of the officers.

'Oh, about three years – give or take a month or two,' Tony put in.

One of the officers, who had been looking round inside

the shack briefly, came out again. 'But there's no water, electricity or plumbing!' he said.

'Sis used the showers and toilets at the mission and she had all her food there,' Bill said. 'She grew some vegetables and took them to the mission to have them cooked. She'd share them round if she had more than she could use.'

'Well, I'll be goddamned,' the officer responded. 'Let's look at this garden. The smell seems to be coming from there.'

'And how!' his colleague replied, fishing in his pocket for a handkerchief to cover his nose.

One of the officers went into the one-room shack to look for some kind of implement with which to start digging, and found an old shovel in a corner. Looking over the garden plot carefully, he found that part of it looked as though it had been recently disturbed. Gagging from the stench, he carefully scraped aside some of the topsoil. There, not far below the surface, in a shallow grave, lay the torso of a woman, minus head and hands.

The officers radioed for backup and told their two informants to stay around as they would be required to answer some questions at headquarters. In short order a squad of detectives arrived, headed by Captain Keith Eads, who took a brief look at the scene of crime and ordered the entire area to be roped off. He then questioned Bill and Tony to find out what they knew about the woman they called 'Sis'.

Captain Eads learned that the church mission was run by a man the regulars knew only as 'Chuck'. While Bill and Tony were taken to headquarters for further questioning, Captain Eads went to the mission and located 'Chuck', whose real name was Charles Pearson. They noted this for their records, but acceded to his request that he be addressed simply as Chuck. He was very shocked to learn that 'Sis' had been found murdered.

He had wondered what had happened to her, and knew that Bill and Tony were intending to go to her woodland abode to see if they could find out anything.

Asked if he knew Sis's real name, Chuck shook his head.

Nobody knew her real name. She never talked about herself or told anyone her name or where she was from. Everyone knew her as Sis. She'd been coming to the mission for about three years and worked in the soup kitchen. Murdered, you say? I can't imagine anyone wanting to murder her! Why, she was just a harmless little old bag lady.

'Old?' queried the Captain. 'She couldn't have been more than thirty!'

'Well,' Chuck said, 'that was just a manner of speaking. It wasn't intended literally.'

'Where do you think she might have come from?'

Chuck replied:

Haven't a clue. She seemed to be very well-spoken, as though she had some education. When she first started coming here she was very well-dressed and seemed to have some money. But when that ran out she managed like all the others, fishing for things in garbage bins and having all her meals here. One of our other regulars used to be a shoemaker and he'd mend her shoes for her. But she wasn't dirty or scruffy like most of the old bag ladies – she kept herself clean and we gave her clothes when she wore hers out.

'How did she keep warm in the winter?' Captain Eads asked. 'In that hut she lived in there's no heating – no electricity, no fireplace, not even a woodstove.'

'She'd stay here until we closed at midnight. I suppose she had blankets and stuff in the hut. Then she'd come back early the next morning.'

He went on to say that at one time he had urged her to

apply for government welfare, as she would then have enough money to enable her to rent a room in a cheap hotel instead of roughing it in the shack. But she had refused, and as far as he knew she had no income and managed like the other street people on what she could find and what she could grow in her little garden. Chuck continued:

> When she first came here I asked her if she had any family. She avoided answering my question and simply told me that she wanted to learn the survival skills of the poor and dispossessed. She had said she disagreed with the exploitation of the consumer society and had dropped out to live a simple life with the street people. She refused government aid because, as she pointed out, the government was committed to spending billions on arms, and she wanted no part of it.

By this time, the detective team had removed the torso to the morgue, and had combed the garden for the missing body parts without success. 'Sis' was labelled in the morgue as a 'Jane Doe', and the forensic pathologists got to work performing an autopsy. The woman had obviously been murdered. Those who die of natural causes or who commit suicide do not cut off their own heads and hands and bury themselves in the garden – as one detective laconically pointed out.

Dr Dennis Troy found numerous slash and stab wounds on the torso indicating a frenzied attack by the killer. Varying depths, widths and shapes of the wounds also appeared to point to a number of different types of knives or other implements having been used in the attack. The head and the hands appeared to have been removed with a saw by someone who was not very conversant with human anatomy and had made a ragged job of it. There had been no sexual assault. The victim, Dr Troy opined, was about thirty years of age, and was white, with dark hair, the colour being ascertained from body hair owing to the absence of the head. In life she would have weighed about 154 pounds (11 stone) and been about 5 ft. 6 in. tall. He estimated that the victim had been dead for about seven days. Dr Troy pointed out that without the head and the hands it would be impossible to attempt to make any identification from dental records or fingerprints.

The absence of these parts also puzzled Captain Eads. A very thorough search of the area had failed to turn up any sign of them. What puzzled the Captain was the motive; robbery was, of course, out of the question, and since the victim had not been sexually assaulted, sex could also be ruled out. The removal of the head and the hands was obviously a ploy to prevent identification. But where were they?

While the autopsy was proceeding, police had lifted the shack bodily from its moorings and hoisted it on to a flatbed pick-up truck. Laboratory-based forensic technicians, examining it, found no evidence pointing to murder: no bloodstains, or implements which could have been used in the killing and dismembering processes. It was apparent that 'Sis' had been lured from her woodland abode and killed elsewhere. Anything that could have identified the victim had been carefully removed; there were no letters, diaries, or anything that could link her to her past life. No personal papers of any kind, which could have borne a name or an address, were to be found. Interestingly, there were a few books of classical English literature – Dickens, Hardy and the like, but there were no names in any of them.

When the fingerprint men dusted items in the shack, only partially smudged prints were lifted, which were useless for identification purposes. Old clothing, blankets, food leftovers and the like were all that could be found. An old mattress on the floor served for a bed, and packing crates and wooden boxes as chairs and tables.

It was thought that a more intensive search for the missing head and hands would be the best course of action to take, as if found they would provide a better chance of identifying the mystery woman. Police contacted the US Navy's Weapons Support Centre and requested the loan of a device known as a thermal imager, which was a sensitive instrument capable of measuring the differences in the temperature of the earth and of flesh buried in it. A team of experts brought the device to police headquarters and scanned the entire area around the crime scene, but failed to find anything.

Eads now turned his attention to the books which had been found in the shack. On the inside cover of one of them he spotted the logo of a bookstore on the campus of Indiana State University. Below this logo, the Captain noticed what looked like a pencil inscription which had been carefully erased. Maybe this might possibly provide a clue?

Eads asked one of the lab technicians to try to 'bring out' the obliterated pencil inscription. He did not really hold out much hope of success, but thought it was worth a try. The technician said he would do what he could with chemicals and the microscope. Eads was quite surprised when the forensic man came up with a clear impression of a name: Ellen Sears Marks. The victim had carefully obliterated it in an effort to sever all links with her past life, little realizing that modern forensic technology would reveal it after her death.

'The only point is,' the Captain mused, 'that she could have picked up the book when scavenging in dumpsters, or even bought it second-hand – in which case we'd be back in square one again.'

Eads called at the office of the university registrar to find out whether they had on their books a student by the name of Ellen Sears Marks who had attended classes there from three to five years earlier. His bid was successful –

the university had a record of an Ellen Sears Marks who had attended as a post-graduate student. She had graduated with honours in English literature and history from the University of Connecticut.

The registrar particularly remembered Ellen Marks because she had surprised everyone by dropping out in the middle of term, although considered to be a brilliant student. Her parents had made a number of unsuccessful attempts to locate her. Eventually they had reported her missing to their local police, who told them that since there was no suspicion of foul play there was nothing they could do. At twenty-five she was an adult and entitled to give up her studies if she wished and relocate elsewhere. With that they had to be content, assuming that Ellen would contact them at some time in the future when she felt ready to do so.

Captain Eads's next port of call was the neat suburban home of Ellen's parents. They were stunned to learn that their daughter was dead, and devastated to know that she had been murdered. Eads told them as gently as he could that he would have to ask them some questions, but offered to come back later for another visit after the initial shock had passed. However, they said they would be prepared to answer Captain Eads's questions on this occasion, to save him from having to make what was a very long trip.

Mr and Mrs Marks told the Captain that they were flabbergasted when the university authorities informed them that their daughter had dropped out in mid-term and had left no forwarding address. Their repeated attempts to locate her all ended in complete deadlock. The local police were unable to help – she was not a 'missing person' in the same way as, for example, a young under-age girl who had run away from home. She had not been abducted from the university or its environs – she had told a number of fellow students that she was increasingly disenchanted with the money-oriented consumer society and wanted to split. She was quoted as having told one friend that she 'was going somewhere to get lost and wanted never to be found'.

Captain Eads asked the grieving parents to let them have any dental records, medical notes such as Ellen's blood group or similar information that would enable them to identify positively the body they had in the morgue. They were able to supply these details. Captain Eads had refrained from telling the parents that their daughter had been decapitated and otherwise mutilated.

With a tentative identification of the torso, Captain Eads now turned his attention to finding her murderer and, if at all possible, why she had been killed. So far, the murder seemed completely motiveless. But some killers, especially those of unstable mind, did commit seemingly pointless crimes, the reasons for which lay buried deep in the darkest recesses of their subconscious mind. Anyway, as Eads told a fellow officer, the main thing now was to catch the murderer; one could then try to unravel his psyche afterwards. A killer who decapitated and mutilated a victim but made no attempt to rape, was a type not unknown among serial killers. It was therefore imperative to apprehend him before he could kill again. But the police were stymied; not a single lead had been forthcoming. It would take a fluke to solve this one.

The fluke came from a most unexpected quarter. One of Captain Eads's detective team came into his office, carrying a case file. 'I thought a lot about this case we're trying to put together,' he said. 'Then I suddenly remembered about a guy I interviewed some little time ago. It sure sounds interesting. Maybe you might like to take a look … ' The officer laid the file on Eads's desk.

It appeared that a man had come to police headquarters to report that he was worried about one of his tenants – 'a real weirdo of the first water', he had called him. The man who had come to the headquarters had identified himself as the proprietor of a rooming-house in one of the seedier parts of town.

One day he was in this tenant's room for the usual weekly cleaning session, when he spotted a notebook lying open on a table. Overcome with curiosity, he read its contents. What he read so perturbed him that he hastily scribbled a copy before his tenant was due to return from work.

The script he copied read, in part: 'Girl or woman must be abducted and killed in a relatively isolated area ... The corpse is to be moved immediately to a place of shelter that is screened and not well-traveled ... ' The script went on to describe various techniques of torture and murder in gruesome detail, including that the victim's head and hands should be cut off and placed in a different location, so that the body could never be identified.

'Bingo!' Captain Eads almost shouted. 'Bring this guy in!' He looked up at the officer who had brought him the file. 'The tenant, of course, not the hotel-keeper.' It seemed that the officer had given Eads a querying look.

Robert Lee, the man in question, was a 31-year-old night clerk in a general store, originally from New York City. When brought in for questioning, he denied all knowledge of Ellen Marks or of any murder. 'I work nights in the store,' he said, 'and I keep myself to myself. I certainly don't mess around with any of the street bums around here.'

A probe into Lee's background revealed that he had faced a rape charge in New York in 1974, but had been acquitted on a technicality. This, however, did not make him a murderer, and the murder victim had not been raped.

At the time that the hotel-keeper had reported his disturbing find to the police, Robert Lee had been questioned, but maintained that the notebook's contents were a preliminary draft for a murder mystery novel he intended writing. The police did not think much of his explanation, taking into consideration that the script was replete with mis-spellings, grammatical errors and an almost complete lack of punctuation. Since the writing of such a script was not illegal, Lee was released. But the detective in charge made a photocopy of it before handing it back to Lee.

Lee's response to questioning this time in connection with the murder of Ellen Marks was to say that he was 'fed up with being hassled just because he had written a murder story'. 'It's not against the law!' he exclaimed in annoyance. 'If it were, half the publishers in America would be out of business!'

The detective who was questioning Lee went to confer with Captain Eads, leaving Lee in the custody of two deputies. 'Guess what!' he told Eads. 'The guy lives in a flophouse not two hundred yards from Ellen Marks's shack! He looks like a prime suspect to me, especially when you think of how the details in his story tally with the way Ellen Marks was killed. I think we should apply for a warrant to search his room and see what we can find.'

Eads agreed, and lost no time in applying to the District Attorney, Ron Walczykowski, for a search warrant. On describing to him the contents of the story in the notebook, Walczykowski replied that it was a 'blueprint for murder'.

Eads himself accompanied the SOCOS (scene-of-crime officers) in a thorough search of the 10 ft.^{2} room where Lee was living. They found eleven knives and a hatchet in the room, but not a bone-cutting saw. However, they turned all the cutlery over to the forensic laboratory for examination. Forensic technicians also examined some stains on the floor and on the porch outside the room, of indeterminate origin. It would take the lab men a few days to ascertain whether these stains were blood or not, and if so, whether they were human blood.

In the meantime, Lee was questioned about his possession of the eleven knives and the hatchet. He maintained that it was not against the law to keep such items at home, just as it was not against the law to write murder stories. He accused the police of 'hassling him for no reason'.

The report from the forensic lab eventually arrived. Not only were the stains of human blood, but the technicians, using chemicals which revealed the presence of blood even if invisible to the naked eye, had discovered a trail of small droplets leading all the way from the porch outside the suspect's room to the shack in which Ellen Marks had led her spartan existence.

After Eads had congratulated the lab men on such thorough and painstaking work which had led to such splendid and conclusive results, Robert Lee was charged with the murder of Ellen Marks. He denied all knowledge of the murder apart from the fact that he had read about it in the papers, and denied that he had ever known her. There were several delays before the trial date could be arranged, but eventually Lee appeared before Judge Kenneth Todd on the first-degree murder charge. He was appointed an attorney by the court, Public Defender Clarence Frank, but Lee elected not to take the stand in his own defence after pleading not guilty.

Eads presented the evidence to Prosecutor Wal-czykowski, who asked whether the victim's head and hands had been found. They had not, but Eads pointed out that they had, perhaps, served a better purpose by going missing, because Lee had obviously carried these parts to his room after killing Ellen Marks and burying her torso in her garden. They had dripped blood, laying a clear trail from the murder scene right to his room. In addition, it was revealed in evidence that a cigarette butt found in the grave beside the torso was of the same brand that Lee smoked, a pack of which had been found in his room. Ellen Marks was a non-smoker.

The public defender objected to the notebook script being put into evidence, but Judge Todd ruled that it was admissible and that the jury could read it. Assistant Prosecutor Stanley Levco presented the state's case. He considered that it was likely that the missing body parts had been placed in plastic garbage bags and put out for collection with household refuse by the sanitation authorities.

At no time did Robert Lee, even to his court-appointed attorney, ever disclose the motive for the killing, or in fact ever admit to having killed Ellen Marks at all.

On Thursday, 18 June 1987, the six-man, six-woman jury, after six hours of deliberation, returned a unanimous verdict of guilty of murder in the first degree with no mitigating circumstances, and Robert Lee was sentenced to sixty years in prison.

5

The Black Dahlia

(Unsolved 1947)

Elizabeth Short was not called the Black Dahlia for nothing. She invariably wore black from head to toe – form-hugging black dresses, black stockings, black high-heeled shoes. Even her hair was raven-black. A beautiful girl, she had green eyes with a shadowy hint of grey.

There was speculation as to whether Elizabeth – or Beth, as she preferred to call herself, wore black at all times as a token of mourning, or whether she wore it because it suited her and made her look glamorous and svelte. She had been engaged to marry a soldier, who had been killed in action in the Second World War. She went to pieces, seeking oblivion in alcohol and drugs. After a time, and some rehabilitation counselling and treatment at a private clinic, she met another man who also offered her marriage, but again a cruel blow of fate destroyed her dreams when he died of a serious illness. Devastated, Beth left for Los Angeles, forsaking her native Massachusetts, and endeavoured to forget her sorrows by throwing herself into a wild life of promiscuity and drink. She did manage to stay off drugs, and in her more lucid moments she turned her efforts to the Hollywood scene, obtaining various small parts in films. It was when she was working as a film extra that she acquired the sobriquet of the Black Dahlia.

On 15 January 1947 an anonymous telephone call came in to the LAPD (Los Angeles Police Department) to say that there was a dead body on some waste ground at the junction of Crenshaw and Santa Barbara Boulevards. The caller hastily rang off, obviously not wishing to become involved: suffice it that he had done his civic duty by reporting his find. Two deputies were hastily despatched to the vacant lot, where they found the body of a young woman, crudely cut in half at the waist. The body was nude, and no clothing of any kind was to be found nearby. Forensic experts called to the scene considered that the victim had been murdered elsewhere and her body transported to the place where it was found, since there was no blood at the scene. The corpse was fresh – her death must have occurred not more than about twenty-four hours before she was found.

The corpse was identified very quickly. Her fingerprints were sent to the FBI in Washington, where they would be on file if she had ever had any brush with the law. She had been arrested as a teenager on a minor juvenile delinquency charge. The report came back identifying her as WF (white female) Elizabeth Short (appropriately 5 ft. 3 in. tall) and weighing 105 pounds (seven and a half stone), born on 29 July 1924 in Hyde Park, Massachusetts.

The call now went out for any information regarding 22-year-old Beth, the beautiful raven-haired, green-eyed girl whose young life had come to such a horrific end. It was soon established that she had acquired the nickname of the Black Dahlia owing to her preference for wearing an all-black ensemble. It was obvious that her killer had known this, because at the autopsy the letters B.D. were found crudely carved on her left thigh. Prior to being cut in half, the girl had possessed film-star looks. Who could possibly have wanted to murder her? There had been no sexual assault. Was it possible that she could have been killed by a rival on the Hollywood scene – a jealous *woman*? It would not have required great strength to kill such a tiny, slender girl. And as a known alcohol abuser, it would have been easy for anyone to slip her a knock-out drug in a drink. A couple of sleeping tablets would have done the job. Curiously, though, the autopsy revealed no trace of drugs in the body, and the amount of alcohol measured in the blood was minimal.

It was discovered that Beth had latterly been down on her luck job-wise and, homeless and penniless, had been staying with a girl friend in San Diego, sleeping on the floor in a blanket because she had sold her sleeping bag to buy food. After this, she was known to have left to meet an airman known as 'Red'. Police quickly located the red-haired serviceman and held him in custody pending questioning, but all that could be established was that he had known her and that the day he had met her was at least five days before her body was found. He was eliminated as a suspect as there was no evidence to tie him to the murder.

A girl who worked as a dance hostess in various Hollywood night clubs recalled seeing Beth six days before she was found, sitting in a bar on South Main Street. The dancer said that Beth had 'sort of an aimless look'. Another girl who knew Beth said that she saw her the same night sitting in the foyer of a local hotel talking earnestly to a young man dressed in workman's overalls. 'They had their heads together,' the girl said. 'They were holding hands and touching each other's hair and the man had an arm round Beth's shoulders.' The witness could not remember the young man's appearance very clearly, apart from how he was dressed.

A bartender in a Hollywood Boulevard bar said that five days before the murder he saw Beth in the company of two girls whom he described as 'of dubious reputation'. Beth, he stated, looked unkempt, as though she had slept in her clothes.

On the following day another bartender, this time in a South Main Street bar, said that he saw Beth and another unidentified girl arguing with two US Navy ratings. Another witness was found who had seen Beth with an unidentified man who booked a room in the hotel he managed on Washington Boulevard.

More witnesses were found who had seen the Black Dahlia only days before her death. One was a bus driver who saw her board his bus at the Santa Barbara bus terminus and alight at the terminus in Los Angeles. This sighting was only about twenty-four hours before her death. That same afternoon she was spotted in a café in San Diego with an unidentified man. No one could be found who could pinpoint her movements between Los Angeles and San Diego. Nor could anyone be found who knew where she was, or with whom, between that time and the following morning when her body was found. It was within that time frame that someone had killed her and transported her body to the vacant lot at the corner of Crenshaw and Santa Barbara Boulevards.

Inquiries by the police at the two bus termini revealed that Beth had left a bag of personal belongings in the left luggage deposit, but when detectives examined its contents, they found nothing of significance in the various letters and diaries. A few letters, written by Beth, sealed and stamped, had never been mailed. The persons named on the envelopes were all interviewed, but it was obvious that they could have had no connection with the murder. The diaries contained few names with identifying details; these, too, were eliminated. Most of the mail sent to Beth care of various friends' addresses had been signed only with a first name or initials, and bore no sender's address. From this, the police deduced that the senders were probably married men.

Since Beth had failed to collect her belongings, which she had deposited only five days before her death, from the bus depot, the police assumed that she had used the facility simply as safe keeping until such time as she found a more permanent base. No money was found in the bag; what little money she had must have been carried in a purse or pocket. No return half bus tickets were found, indicating that she had no settled abode. Her last address known to the police was in Santa Barbara, but inquiries there drew a blank. Nobody had seen her there for several weeks.

The investigations into the various persons named in the letters and diaries were proceeding, when a letter packet was received by a Los Angeles daily newspaper. Both the address on the envelope and the missive inside were composed with words clipped from newspapers. The packet contained Beth's birth certificate, a little black book containing various names and addresses which had been known to be carried by her, a newspaper cutting about the marriage of a former boyfriend, and a baggage reclaim ticket for the case left at the bus deposit office – the case which the police had already examined. The message which came with these items read simply: HERE ARE BLACK DAHLIA'S BELONGINGS. LETTER TO FOLLOW.

The next day, as promised, the follow-up letter arrived. It read: TURNING MYSELF IN, WEDNESDAY, 29 JANUARY, 10 A.M.. It was signed: THE BLACK DAHLIA AVENGER. Both the note and the envelope had again been made up from newsprint. The police dusted both this and the earlier communication for fingerprints, but none could be lifted. The items enclosed with the first letter were also tested, but they had been wiped clean. Not even the fingerprints of the Black Dahlia herself remained.

The police did not consider these letters to be the work of a hoaxer, because of the fact that items belonging to the dead girl had been enclosed. It is most unlikely that someone else who had known her would have gained access to them, in particular her little black book, which she guarded jealously and kept with her at all times. Detectives working on the case were, however, somewhat puzzled that the sender had included the left luggage reclaim ticket, and not attempted to use it himself to obtain Beth's deposited belongings from the bus terminus.

It is not unusual for a psychotic killer to send communications to the newspapers or to the police, apparently to taunt them; Jack the Ripper himself started the trend. What was not clear was why the sender should have dubbed himself the Black Dahlia Avenger. What did he have to avenge? No one who had known Beth could even begin to hazard a guess. All the police could do at this point was to bide their time until 10 a.m. on Wednesday to see if he would give himself up. Most of the officers thought that he would not.

On the Tuesday night previous to the anticipated surrender, a man by the name of Voorhees went to police headquarters and told them that he had killed the Black Dahlia and wanted to give himself up, saying that he could no longer stand the suspense. He made a confession which was so at variance with the known facts that it was immediately seen for what it was – the disordered fantasy of a man with a sick mind. It was proved that he could never have even known the dead girl. He was released the same night with a recommendation that he attend a psychiatrist's clinic. Voorhees was but the first of many such who made false confessions – the bizarre case had sparked off a chain reaction. All were thoroughly checked out and dismissed out of hand. None of them could have had even the remotest connection with the murder.

Ten o'clock on Wednesday came, but none of the

officers at the LAPD headquarters was exactly holding his breath. By this time all had come round to the opinion that the sender of the letters would not turn up. And they were absolutely right. However, the next day another newsprint note arrived, saying: HAVE CHANGED MY MIND. SORRY TO DISAPPOINT YOU. It was again signed THE BLACK DAHLIA AVENGER. That was the last communication the Los Angeles newspapers, or the police, ever received from this source.

The case of the Black Dahlia remains unsolved to this day. A beautiful, slender reed of a girl met a hideous death twenty-five years ago, and still no one knows why.

6

Draw the Well Dry

Pierre Voirbo (1869)

The restaurant was situated in the rue Princesse, a side street off the Boulevard St Germaine in Paris. The owner-manager, a Monsieur Dufy, did not live on the premises but in a house a few doors away.

A diner poured water from the carafe on the table into the glass and raised it to his lips. A peculiar odour wafted to his nostrils. He put the glass down and called for M. Dufy. 'This water smells most odd,' he said. 'Bring me a bottle of wine instead.' M. Dufy tipped the contents of the glass back into the carafe, removed it and brought the wine. 'I hope this is more to your liking, Monsieur,' he said. He took the carafe and poured the water down the sink.

The kitchen hand looked up from peeling potatoes. 'The water is off,' he said. 'I was going to drink some, but thought better of it.'

'Rubbish!' exclaimed the manager. 'There's nothing wrong with it. Tends to smell a bit stronger at this time of year, that's all.'

Later that same evening, another diner had gone so far as to taste the water in his carafe. Hastily he spat it out into his table napkin. *'Mon Dieu!'* he spluttered. 'The water is foul!'

M. Dufy came running out of the kitchen. He took one sniff. 'It certainly is not as fresh as it could be,' he said. 'I will bring you a bottle of wine instead, Monsieur. On the house.'

After thus pacifying the customer, M. Dufy thought that would be the last of it. But no. Over the next day or two, complaints increased. M. Dufy was pouring the contents of more and more carafes down the sink, and the kitchen hand kept giving him a knowing look, as though to say, 'I told you so,' although he considered it prudent not to annoy his employer by voicing his opinion. Let the water speak for itself …

In 1869 there was no piped water. All the water had to be drawn from the well in the courtyard. M. Dufy deemed it an urgent priority to examine the well and take a sample of the water before he lost any more customers. As he went out to the well with a vessel to sample the water, he spotted Alphonse, the kitchen hand, eyeing him with a smug look on his face. 'Get on with your work!' he ordered tersely. He did not want to look a fool before his kitchen staff.

When M. Dufy reached the well, which was a large one and 60 ft. deep, he lifted the metal grid which covered the top to prevent dead leaves and dust from falling into the water. He did not need to dip the vessel into the water to take a sample; a large object was floating on the surface, and the nauseating odour emanating from this object left M. Dufy in no doubt that this was the source of the noisome pollution. He went back indoors and fetched a long pole with a hook at one end, used for reaching high windows to open and close them. With a little difficulty, he managed to hook the floating object over the side of the well and on to the ground. It was all too obvious what it was: a human lower leg, encased in a stocking.

'*Merde!*' the restaurateur cried as he hastily dropped the pole and, leaving the leg on the ground, rushed round the corner to the local branch of the Sûreté. 'There's part of a human body in my well!' he gasped. 'Send an officer!'

The gendarme in the reception office told M. Dufy to calm himself. A policeman would accompany him back to the restaurant immediately. The officer sent to go with him was Gustave Macé, at that time not yet known throughout France as he later would be when he became head of the Paris Sûreté and one of the most astute detectives ever to investigate crime in France.

Macé borrowed the long pole and fished in the well to see if there were any more body parts, and he was not really surprised to discover another package floating just below the surface. On closer examination, this proved to be another human lower leg. As well as a stocking, it was also encased in a piece of black glazed calico. This was sewn along its length, but had become unfastened at one end leaving enough space to have accommodated another leg. It seemed, therefore, that the parcel had originally contained both legs, but that when the stitching had given way the other stockinged leg had worked loose. It was obvious that the legs had been in the water for some time, since the escape of gases would have caused them to rise and float at or near the surface, and the process of decomposition would have tended to weaken and eventually rot the thread used to sew the parcel together.

Doctors who performed an autopsy on the severed legs decided that they were those of a man not younger than fifty years of age and possibly much older. They considered that the body parts had been in the water for about six weeks. Looking through their files for any possible leads, the police had a record of a human thigh which had been fished from the Seine a few days before

Christmas. It was now almost the end of January. If the thigh belonged to the same body as the legs, that would have added up to approximately six weeks, the doctors' estimate. The femur from another human thigh had turned up at about the same time in a gutter in the rue Jacob, not far from where the complete thigh had been found. These parts were taken to the morgue, and at that time were thought to be the result of a prank by medical students who had been dissecting a cadaver. Such happenings were not unknown.

Things now began to look rather different. Pathologists now compared the severed lower legs with the thigh and the femur from the morgue, and soon found that they matched, tissue for tissue, bone for bone. The legs were those of the same individual whose thighs had been also part of a dismembering process. But where was the torso? The head would be very helpful for identification purposes, as would the arms – or at least the hands for fingerprinting. An extensive police search failed to find parts or parcels from what the gendarmes had now dubbed 'the old man of the morgue'. And, more important, who was the victim and who had killed him?

Macé discovered that the way the black calico parcel had been sewn together was a method of stitching used by tailors and tailoresses. He also discovered a mark sewn into the top of one of the stockings – +B+ – which was not a laundry mark. During the course of his investigations covering this angle, a laundry proprietor informed Macé that he had seen a man throwing what looked like pieces of meat into the river, while he (the laundryman) was out for a walk along the bank. After the customary greeting, he had asked the man what he was doing, and he replied that he was baiting for fish. 'I thought the pieces of meat were a bit big for bait,' the witness told the investigator, 'but thought nothing of it. I never said anything. After all, if he couldn't be bothered to cut up the joints into smaller pieces for bait, that was his problem.'

Macé thought privately that the 'fisherman' had a much bigger problem than baiting for fish. There was not much to fish for in the Seine anyway; it was much too polluted. All kinds of refuse was hurled into the river by the locals, not to mention the raw sewage that was channelled into it as a matter of course. Any self-respecting fish would be dead long ago. Still, it was not part of a policeman's routine to discuss his suspicions with witnesses; that was more the kind of thing to be mulled over at headquarters. A report was duly made. Unfortunately the laundryman's walk had been at night, and it was impossible for him to describe the 'fisherman' as it had been completely dark, although he did think the man was not particularly tall.

A further search of records on file revealed that a day or two after the laundryman's sighting of the 'fisherman' a man had been stopped by the police in the early hours carrying a parcel and looking furtively around as he walked along. Police naturally suspected that he was a burglar making off with his loot. The man explained that he had just arrived in Paris by the night train and, unable to find a cab, had set out to walk to his destination. Asked what the parcel contained, he said that it was a ham. The man 'looked like an honest type', according to one of the two officers who had questioned him, who obviously did not think it unusual for a man to be wandering around at one o'clock in the morning carrying a ham but no other luggage, although he had just got off the Paris night express. As for his furtive looking around, he said he was, after all, looking out for a cab.

Macé studied this report and questioned the two gendarmes who had been on street patrol in the area. 'Where did this incident take place?' he asked.

'Oh, it was just a little way from the rue Princesse, just off the Boulevard St Germaine,' he was told.

The rue Princesse? That was the street where M. Dufy

had found the legs in his well. It looked very much as though the man had panicked from the shock of such a close shave with the police and had hastily dumped the 'ham' in the well as he skirted the courtyard. It would seem that he was a local – or at least knew the area. Macé asked the two policemen to describe him. 'Shortish, of stocky build and round-faced with a moustache,' they told him. That would just about tally with the laundryman's description of a man who was not very tall, even if he had not seen his face clearly in the dark. The policemen, unlike the laundryman, had carried lanterns.

Macé's next task was to try to find a tailor, or tailoress, who could have been the person who stitched the legs into a parcel of calico, even if he or she had not actually been the murderer of 'the old man of the morgue'. M. Dufy told the investigator that a tailoress named Mathilde Gaupe lived in the flat above the restaurant, paying him rent for her tenancy. She had a number of friends who visited her, including acquaintances who asked her to do tailoring work for them. M. Dufy was asked whether Mlle Gaupe had any male visitors who were below average height, round-faced with a moustache and of stocky build. 'Why, yes, sir,' was the reply. 'That sounds like Pierre Voirbo. He's a tailor, too. He's also a political activist – a radical. Always trying to stir things up at political meetings ... '

The physical description was enough for Gustave Macé; he was not really concerned that he fancied himself as a revolutionary. Left-wing firebrands were all too common in France. But they did not all visit Mlle Gaupe, nor were they tailors. He obtained the address of M. Voirbo and paid him a visit.

Voirbo was a voluble, back-slapping, hail-fellow-well-met type who was adept at bluffing his way out of most sticky situations. He welcomed the policeman and offered him coffee. He had recently moved to this new abode, he told Macé, as it was more spacious and thus allowed more room for his sewing-machine and other accoutrements of his trade.

Asked by Voirbo the reason for his visit, Macé told him that some body parts had been found sewn with tailor's stitching into a bag, and he was interviewing all tailors in the area, both male and female. Voirbo did not bat an eyelid. He remained as cool as the proverbial cucumber.

On the way out, Macé asked Voirbo casually where he had moved from. He told him: 2 rue Mazarine. Macé decided to visit Voirbo's old lodgings.

The concierge told the investigator that Voirbo was a semi-recluse with few friends, his main companion being an old man, 72-year-old Désiré Bodasse, a retired upholsterer, with whom he spent most of his time drinking, either in his room or at the local tavern. She added that Voirbo was one of the most untidy and slovenly tenants she had ever had to put up with. There had, however, been one very strange incident. On 17 December – she remembered the date because it had been her birthday – she had gone as usual to clean his room, and found that it had been scrubbed from top to bottom. She found him bustling about rearranging furniture and rugs. Asked why he had cleaned his room when it was her due day to come and do it for him, he had told her that he had spilt some strong-smelling fluid he used for his work and he had done a thorough cleaning job to get rid of the smell.

By now Macé was certain that he had his man. He also knew the identity of the victim – Désiré Bodasse. It remained for him to make a few inquiries about *him*.

Désiré Bodasse was an ageing roué with an eye for the ladies, especially those in their late teens and early twenties. One of the reasons he was always hanging around in Voirbo's workshop, the concierge had said, was to try his chances with some of Voirbo's young assistant tailoresses and pressers, usually with singular lack of success, since the young ladies preferred fellows in their own age-group, not a man of seventy-two.

Bodasse was fairly well off, having saved assiduously when he was working, and owing to his miserly disposition he had amassed a tidy sum – about 10,000 francs, which he had prudently invested in Italian government stock. This was issued in the form of pay-to-bearer securities, which could be used as legal tender, like banknotes. Being consecutively numbered, they were much less vulnerable to theft. Bodasse kept them well hidden and, in addition, he kept a note of their numbers on a piece of paper folded small and inserted into the back of his gold watch. He did not wear the watch on a chain, as a precaution against 'dippers' – a translation of the French for 'pickpockets'. He kept the watch in his room, hanging over his bed. His friend Pierre Voirbo was certainly aware of his financial assets.

Macé turned up witnesses who had overheard Voirbo and Bodasse talking in the local tavern. In their cups, the conversation was invariably about wine and women – if not much song. During one such conversation, Voirbo was heard to tell Bodasse that at thirty-one it was time he married and had a prospective fiancée in mind, but was short of money; could his friend let him have a loan? Bodasse had refused.

On another occasion, when Voirbo raised the subject of marriage, Bodasse had told him not to saddle himself with the responsibility of a family but to enjoy his freedom. 'Look at me,' Bodasse said, 'a bachelor gay all my life. How else do you think I could have saved money? A wife and children would have taken the lot!' Voirbo had replied that different men had different temperaments and preferred different lifestyles. Bodasse retorted that this marriage lark was all just a ploy to try to induce him to give him a loan, and that once Voirbo had the money he might not marry anyway!

Yet another witness said that Bodasse had dropped out of sight some six or seven weeks previously and no one had seen him either in the tavern or on the street. Voirbo had still spent time drinking there, but alone.

By now Macé was fully convinced that Voirbo had murdered Bodasse for his money. He would have had no problem at all in luring the old man to his workshop – he would only have had to tell him a new employee – a blonde – was starting work there that day, and Bodasse would have been there like a shot.

Macé decided that the most likely place, therefore, where his suspect could have murdered Bodasse, was in his old lodgings. He went to interview the concierge again and asked her to tell him how Voirbo had paid up his rent before leaving. The woman told Macé that Voirbo had paid her with Italian government pay-to-bearer negotiable securities. That clinched it: he must have discovered Bodasse's hidden hoard after the murder. Macé asked the woman to show him the room Voirbo had occupied. There was a large table in the middle of the room – a table more than big enough to stretch out a human body. The astute and observant detective also noticed something that might well have escaped a lesser mortal – a depression in the floor under the table, where a few of the quarry tiles had been laid somewhat unevenly and sloped slightly to the centre. It was not much of a depression, but it was there.

Macé decided not to brook another moment's delay – he now had his case. He took Voirbo, accompanied by two gendarmes, to his old lodgings, and the four of them were admitted up the stairs to the suspect's old room which had served as both living quarters and workshop. A chair was drawn up and Voirbo told to sit on it to watch a demonstration which would prove that the room had also been the scene of a murder and dismemberment of the victim's body.

Macé took a carafe of water and poured it on to the surface of the table. The water ran over the edge of the table and on to the tiled floor below, where it quickly ran into the depression, the force of gravity impelling it down the slight slope, and collected in a puddle in the centre, gradually seeping through the cracks in the tiles. Macé pronounced in his best lecture-room voice:

> Blood would have behaved in the same way. It would have collected on the tiles under the middle of the table. And because of the depression in the floor at that point, it would have run through the cracks in the floor caused by the spaces between the tiles. We shall only need to lift some of these tiles, and we shall certainly find traces of blood beneath them. However well-scrubbed the upper surfaces were, the murderer would not have lifted the tiles and washed them, too.

Voirbo, seated a few feet from this masterly demonstration, paled visibly and strove to keep himself from trembling as Macé ordered the gendarmes, who had come prepared with the necessary tools to prise up the tiles from the middle of the floor under the big wooden table. And, as surely as night follows day, Macé's prediction had come true. The undersides of all the tiles in the middle of the floor under the table were caked with dried blood, as was the cement bedding over which they had been laid.

Voirbo jumped from his chair, sweating. 'I am guilty!' he gasped. 'I will tell you all! But take me out of this accursed place.' Thus Macé had extracted a confession from the killer before he had even been charged.

Voirbo cheated the guillotine. While he languished in prison awaiting trial, someone smuggled a razor to him in a loaf of bread, and he cut his throat.

7

The Bad Neighbour

Louis Voisin (1917)

The word *voisin* means 'neighbour' in French, but Louis Voisin was not a very good neighbour. In fact he was a very bad one, since he murdered his mistress who lived next door.

Like Pierre Voirbo in the preceding chapter, Louis Voisin was a Frenchman, but there the resemblance ends. Unlike Voirbo, who was short and slightly-built, Louis Voisin was a big, burly, red-faced, beefy fellow of forty-two living in London, where he followed his trade as a butcher in Soho.

On 2 November 1917 a roadsweeper performing his duties in Regent Square, Bloomsbury, spotted a bundle tied in sacking lying just inside the railings of the gardens which were situated in the middle of the square. Naturally he was curious – quite apart from the fact that it was part of his job to clear dumped rubbish away from the gardens.

On investigation the man was horrified to discover that the bundle contained the torso and arms of a woman. She had been decapitated, and her hands had been cut off. The roadsweeper dropped his brush and hastened from the square to find a constable.

The policeman, half-disbelieving the man's claim that he had 'found a body', was soon disabused of his scepticism, and on making a preliminary search of the area he quickly found a second bundle. This was a brown paper parcel containing a woman's legs. The police station was not far away and a detachment of officers soon arrived to cordon off the area and make a fuller investigation. After some questioning, the council workman, white and shaken, was allowed to continue with his work.

In the mortuary, the remains were quickly traced from a laundry mark on a sheet in which the torso had been wrapped before being bundled into a meat sack. On the brown paper which wrapped the legs, someone had scrawled the words 'Blodie Belgiam' in a semi-literate hand. The laundry mark 11-H pinpointed the sheet as having belonged to a Mme Émilienne Gérard, aged thirty-two, who lived in a flat not far away. She had been missing for three days; no one had seen her since 31 October.

Police searching her flat found an IOU for £50 signed by Louis Voisin, whose portrait also stood on the mantelpiece, signed with the same name. Police correctly surmised that Louis Voisin was, or had been, the dead woman's lover.

Inquiries elicited the fact that Louis Voisin lived next door – he was the neighbour of the deceased in name as well as location. He was not at home when the police called, and they were told that he could be found at 101 Charlotte Street, where he had a butcher's shop with a basement flat beneath. Hastening there, the police found Voisin sitting at the kitchen table in this basement flat with another Frenchwoman, Berthe Roche. Asked when he had last seen Mme Gérard, he said that it was on the evening of 31 October when she had told him she was going over to France for a few days to visit relatives in Paris.

The police suspected Voisin right from the start. There were bloodstains aplenty in his basement kitchen, but he averred that the blood was that of a calf he had slaughtered. Asked if he usually slaughtered animals in his kitchen instead of using the abattoir, he put forth the feeble excuse that 'the calf was making so much noise that I thought it best to knock it off on the spot'. What Voisin did not know was that forensic science had progressed to the point where it was a simple matter to differentiate human blood from animal blood, and that no less august a personage than the great Bernard Spilsbury would disprove his statement. Police suspicion of Voisin was already reinforced by the fact that Spilsbury, at the autopsy, had stated that the head, hands and legs had been dismembered with the skill of a butcher who knew precisely where to cut through the joints. The fact that the torso was found encased in a meat sack also strengthened the evidence pointing to murder by a butcher.

The police took Voisin and Berthe Roche in for questioning without further ado, and while they were in custody they searched the basement flat beneath the butcher's shop. In one corner stood a barrel, and when this was opened it was found to contain, buried in sawdust, the missing head and hands of the unfortunate Émilienne Gérard. These parts had obviously been hidden in an attempt to prevent identification. What puzzled the police, however, was the significance of the words 'Blodie Belgiam' scrawled on the brown paper that had wrapped the legs. It would seem, on the face of it, that it was a crude attempt to mislead the police, by implying that the victim was, in the murderer's opinion, 'a bloody Belgian'. Mme Gérard was French and had never even been to Belgium, nor did she have any connections there.

At the police station Voisin was asked to write the words 'Bloody Belgian' for comparison with the writing on the paper. He wrote 'Blodie Belgiam' in the same illiterate scrawl.

Louis Voisin was charged by Chief Inspector Wensley with the murder of Émilienne Gérard, and Berthe Roche was charged with being an accessory before the fact. Spilsbury said that the dead woman had been knocked unconscious with what he described as 'some fairly light blows' before having her throat cut. The police surmised that when Mme Gérard visited Voisin at his butcher's establishment and found him there with his new mistress, the two women came to blows. In the scuffle Mme Gérard knocked Berthe Roche unconscious with blows to the head, and Voisin then delivered the *coup de grâce* by cutting her throat, thus disposing of the discarded mistress who was 'in the way' and leaving him free to direct his attentions towards Berthe Roche.

Voisin, in custody, hotly denied this assumption. He stated that he had gone to visit Mme Gérard to settle up the IOU for £50 that had been found in her flat, and found her lying dead on the floor. He said he had no idea how she had died. He thought it unlikely that she would have had a heart attack or otherwise died from natural causes at thirty-two, nor did he think she would have committed suicide. He supposed that an intruder had killed her – possibly a burglar who had thought the flat empty.

Voisin then went on to say that he panicked and cut up the body so as to dispose of it. Asked why he had not just called the police, he said, 'It would have looked very bad for me, with her lying dead like that. The police might have thought it was me.' Wensley suppressed a smile at the curious implication caused by the Frenchman's ungrammatical construction.

The cock-and-bull story put up by the butcher did not cut any ice with Chief Inspector Wensley, and Louis

Voisin and Berthe Roche were sent for trial at the Old Bailey in January 1918. In his defence Voisin repeated the same improbable story he had told the police, but judge and jury alike dismissed it as pure fantasy. Voisin was sentenced to death, and his trial was unique in that it was the only case on record in which the judge pronounced the sentence of death in French – the language of the defendant. The actual court proceedings had been conducted in English, but had been translated for him by a court official. He was hanged in Pentonville Prison on 2 March 1918.

Berthe Roche was sentenced to seven years' penal servitude, but two years afterwards she went insane and died in prison on 22 May 1919.

8

A Shock for the Plumber

Dennis Nilsen (1983)

Tuesday, 8 February was just a day like any other to Mike Cattran, an employee of the Dyno-Rod plumbing firm. He'd been called out to unblock sinks, clear pipes and dislodge soft toys which had been stuffed down a toilet by a 2-year-old. All in a day's work. But the last call of the day, in the evening just as he was preparing to go home, was something else again. It was a call-out he'd never forget.

The call came in to send a plumber to 23 Cranley Gardens, Muswell Hill, in North London. All the tenants of the house, which was divided into flats, had been complaining that since the preceding Saturday they had been unable to flush their toilets. There was some kind of blockage which affected the whole system that served the flats.

The tenant of the ground floor flat showed Cattran the location of the manhole cover that led down to the sewage system. When the plumber lifted the cover, he was almost knocked off his feet by a nauseating stench. It was patently obvious that rotting meat was the source of the smell. Someone had, it seemed, attempted to dispose of some rotting meat by trying to flush it down the toilet instead of putting it out in the dustbin wrapped in plenty of newspaper.

Cattran tied a wet towel (provided by the ground floor tenant) over his nose and mouth and proceeded to descend the iron steps into the black depths, torch in hand. The tenant had meanwhile made a hasty retreat, understandably enough.

Flashing his torch around, Cattran soon discovered the source of the smell. Rotting white meat – chicken, or perhaps pork. But it looked rather odd. There were some strange shapes among this meat – shapes that looked suspiciously like fingers. Chicken or pork didn't have fingers. Cattran decided to ring his supervisor for instructions, and was told that the supervisor would come first thing in the morning next day, as he had already gone home. So the plumber climbed back to terra firma and told the ground floor tenant that help would be arriving at 8 a.m. the next day to deal with matters.

The supervisor arrived duly at eight o'clock and prepared to go down into the system to check the obstruction. To his astonishment, he found that most of it had been cleared, but the odour was still in evidence – slightly lessened in intensity, though not much. The Dyno-Rod supervisor decided to question the tenants of the flats to see if they could throw any light on the cause of the blockage and also how it had managed to clear itself during the night.

One tenant told him that she had been kept awake most of the night by the noise of footsteps going up and down the stairs to and from the flat on the uppermost floor, which was known as the 'Top Flat'. No one else had heard anything. Maybe they were not such light sleepers as the lady in question. In the meantime, plumbing engineers were re-examining the sewer below ground, and they found that the pipe was not completely clear but still partly blocked. The obstruction looked like no kind of chicken or pork that the men had ever seen. They both thought it looked like human flesh, including fingers and bones. This was a case for calling the police, said the supervisor – and he did.

Detective Chief Inspector Peter Jay, of Hornsey CID, came to inspect the sewer. This time it was his turn to borrow a wet towel. He also interviewed the lady who had reported hearing the ascending and descending footsteps that had kept her awake all night. She told him, in answer to his question, that the tenant of the 'Top Flat' was a civil servant named Dennis Nilsen, who was out all day at work but usually arrived home in the evenings around six o'clock. When Nilsen arrived home that night, he found DCI Peter Jay waiting for him in the ground floor hall.

Dennis Nilsen was a 37-year-old office worker at the Jobcentre in Denmark Street, in Soho, London. DCI Jay came straight to the point and told Nilsen that he wanted to talk to him about the problem with the sewer. Nilsen invited the detective up to his flat, and as soon as he entered it the policeman knew that Nilsen held the key to the mystery of how human remains had become wedged in the sewer pipe, for the same odour permeated the flat that he had been subjected to in the sewer, overlaid by the smell of disinfectant which had obviously been sprayed around in an attempt to mask the odour, not very successfully. He had no wet towel with him this time …

'I believe you know how those human remains came to be in the sewage system,' DCI Jay told Nilsen. 'What happened to the rest of the body?'

Nilsen looked at the detective without batting an eyelid. He pointed to the wardrobe. 'It's in there,' he said in a matter-of-fact voice. 'In two black plastic rubbish-bags.'

Nilsen was taken to Hornsey Police Station for

questioning. On the way, DCI Jay asked him if the remains in the bags and in the drains were those of one body or two. Nilsen immediately replied, 'There have been fifteen or sixteen altogether.' His remark was made in a completely detached manner, quite devoid of any sign of emotion.

Once in the police station, Nilsen spilled his guts. He talked, and he talked, and he talked. Hardened policemen could not believe what they were hearing, and not a few experienced detectives thought at first that Nilsen was one of those compulsive confessors who turn up from time to time. Although he had obviously killed a man, or men, they thought he was embroidering his account to 'look big', as such murderers often do, or maybe to shock – all part of the psychopath's psychological makeup.

Nilsen told the detectives that he had killed three men in his Cranley Gardens flat, and that he had killed another twelve or thirteen – he couldn't remember which – in the house he had lived in at 195 Melrose Avenue, Cricklewood, over a five-year period. 'I'm not absolutely sure of the number,' he said. 'I didn't keep a body count.'

In the meantime, police searching Nilsen's Cranley Gardens flat discovered three severed heads in plastic bags in the wardrobe and dismembered parts of three bodies in a tea chest in the flat. Forensic examination revealed that two of the three heads had had much of the flesh stripped off and that they had in fact been boiled. In addition to the three heads and the material in the tea chest, searchers also found the entire lower half of a torso in the bathroom. This was found to match up to body parts found in the tea chest. After all this evidence had been removed and the drainage system completely cleared, men were detailed to cleanse and disinfect both the flat and the drains, and to assure tenants that they could now flush their toilets with impunity. Not all the tenants stayed to do so, however – one moved out lock, stock and barrel the very next day to stay with relatives, while another gave notice to the landlord that he would be going as soon as he could find another flat. At the other extreme, crowds of morbid sightseers flocked to see the house, and were moved on by police. It was some considerable time before Cranley Gardens returned to any semblance of normality. Eventually all the tenants moved out and the house was put up for sale in 1983. There were few prospective purchasers and it was more than a year before the house was eventually sold at a price well below its market value.

Nilsen had moved in the autumn of 1981 to the Cranley Gardens flat, and the job which had so shocked Mike Cattran the plumber was carried out on 8 February 1983. Thus, Nilsen's last three victims were all killed over about a year and a half. The police now turned their attention to the house at 195 Melrose Avenue in Cricklewood, where Nilsen said he had killed 'twelve or thirteen' other victims. The house was searched and the garden dug up. No evidence was found in the house itself, but the garden yielded plenty. Teams of police diggers took almost a fortnight to complete the job, and unearthed quantities of human remains. Bones from numerous bodies were dug up in the garden, while suitcases containing human remains had been stowed in a garden shed which still stood, locked and padlocked but not used by the subsequent tenants, whose tenancy had obviously obliterated all traces of blood or other evidence from the interior of the house itself, since over an approximately seventeen-month period floors and other surfaces would have been scrubbed many times.

Scots-born Nilsen started life on 23 November 1945. After leaving high school he joined the Army, from which he was discharged in 1972. During his twelve years' service he had been a cook in the catering corps and had seen action in Aden, Sharjah on the Gulf, Cyprus and finally West Germany. After his discharge he joined the Metropolitan Police, but found the life not to his liking and resigned after only eleven months. He then took a job as a security guard, working for the Department of the Environment, but that, too, did not appeal to him: he never met anybody and felt very lonely and isolated. The fact that he was a homosexual did not help matters; he was on duty at times when he could have cruised the gay bars. So finally he took a clerical position at the Jobcentre in which he was working at the time of his arrest. There he had plenty of opportunity to meet the disadvantaged, the drop outs and the unemployed who felt rejected and carried a chip on their shoulder. After working hours he would go home, change and cook himself a meal, then head for the West End bars in search of the young male company he craved.

Up to 1975 Nilsen had been living in Teignmouth Road, Willesden, in north-west London, and it was in that year that he met an Irishman ten years his junior named David Gallichan, and eventually decided to share a flat. Although the flatmates started their sharing relationship at the Teignmouth Road address, they soon realized that the flat was far too small for two, and looked for a larger abode. This they found at 195 Melrose Avenue, Cricklewood, to which they moved in November 1975. Nilsen found the round of cosy domesticity to be just what he needed, offering security, companionship and warmth. Nilsen did all the cooking, David tended the garden, and they acquired a dog and a cat. David worked as a railway porter, and Nilsen enjoyed his clerical job, and it seems unlikely that if this state of affairs had continued, Nilsen would ever have become a serial killer.

But the idyll was not to last. In May 1977 David Gallichan was offered a job in the country working for an antique dealer, which he quickly accepted, explaining that he had always had a yearning to live in a rural setting.

When he left, Nilsen was devastated – his secure world had collapsed like a burst balloon. On the face of it, it would seem that Gallichan's feelings for his flatmate were less intense than the other way round. Nilsen took refuge in drink.

Nilsen's initial shock soon turned to anger, but it was a controlled kind of rage, an inner fury that manifested itself in taciturnity and cold aloofness. Only when well loaded with hard liquor did he mellow sufficiently to allow his normally talkative, expansive self to surface.

In the Cricklewood Arms Nilsen was garrulous in his cups and had little difficulty in talking a young Irishman, whose identity has never been ascertained, into coming home with him on the night of 30 December 1978. The intention was to keep his companion with him over the New Year period, but the Irishman had other ideas. However, he was perfectly amenable to staying the night with Nilsen and indulging in homosexual behaviour, although he had made it clear that he would be leaving the following morning. Nilsen, however, had no intention of letting him do so. He strangled him with his tie at some time during that night. In his later confession, he averred that he 'had no recollection' of the act and had awakened in the early hours 'to discover that he had strangled him in his sleep'. Few believed him. Afterwards, he said, he carefully washed the body in the bath, put it back in bed and sexually abused it. 'I now had a new flatmate,' he later said. 'I had the company I needed.' After re-dressing the corpse and masturbating over it, he prised up the floorboards, wrapped the clothed body in two black plastic rubbish bags, and laid it under the floorboards, where it remained for an incredible seven-and-a-half months after which time Nilsen removed it from its makeshift grave and burned it on a bonfire in the garden, heaping a number of rubber car tyres on top so that the smell of burning rubber would mask the odour of burning flesh.

Nilsen's reaction to the realization that he had actually killed a fellow human being was a severe attack of nerves. He later told police that he 'shook uncontrollably' for several hours, and debated in his mind whether or not to commit suicide. He then considered giving himself up to the police. Eventually he decided that if he took either course there would be no one to look after his dog, of which he was very fond. He said that he was amazed that no one came to see him or question him about the matter.

Nilsen did, however, have a brief run-in with the law on 31 October 1979. He had picked up a young Chinese student, Andrew Ho, in a pub near Trafalgar Square called the Salisbury. After a few drinks at the flat, Nilsen attempted to strangle him with a tie, but the student managed to break free and grabbed a brass candlestick with which he managed to knock Nilsen out before making good his escape. He feared that he might have killed his assailant and went to the police. On investigation Nilsen said that he had been drunk and did not remember anything, and no charges were made. 'That was cutting things a bit close,' Nilsen said in his later statement. But it did not stop him from continuing to lure victims to his flat with deadly intentions ...

Nilsen's second victim was a 23-year-old Canadian student named Kenneth Ockenden. He was not gay, but was pleased to meet Nilsen and accept drinks from him, this time in the Princess Louise pub in High Holborn. This was but the prelude to a heavy drinking session at the flat, interspersed with a meal of ham, eggs and chips cooked by Nilsen. Nilsen played a number of rock-'n'-roll tapes, to which he persuaded his new companion to listen on headphones. Moving behind him on the pretext of fetching more booze from the kitchen, Nilsen strangled him with the headphone cord. For some reason, Nilsen said, they did not engage in any sexual activities beyond touching and caressing. Nilsen propped the body up in an armchair in front of the TV and talked to it as though it were alive. Finally he washed the body, as he did with all his victims, and made up the dead face with cosmetics and shampooed its hair. After a day or two the corpse was laid to rest under the floorboards, but Nilsen took it out again no fewer than four times over the ensuing fourteen days, each time having intercrural sex (i.e. between the thighs) with his dead companion.

In the course of undressing the body, Nilsen discovered that Kenneth Ockenden had a large quantity of money in Canadian dollars, secreted in a money belt. Nilsen tore the bills in pieces and burned them. Stealing was not his scene at all. Later, when he was found to be wearing a gold watch which had belonged to one of his victims, he told police, 'Its owner had not really gone away, so it was not theft.' Indeed it was true in a sense, for that victim was still under the floorboards at the time.

After this, his second murder, Nilsen stated that he still felt 'bewildered and frightened by his own actions' and again considered the same two options that he had addressed previously, but soon afterwards found that he was becoming what he termed 'less emotional' about the whole thing. He was beginning to think that he could kill with impunity.

Martyn Duffy, a Liverpool-Irish youth of sixteen already heavily into alcohol and drugs, was Nilsen's next victim. He also had a record for petty theft. It was May of 1980 when Nilsen took the boy to his flat, strangled him, washed the body in the bath, masturbated over it and laid him under the floorboards by the side of the unfortunate Kenneth Ockenden. The odours of decomposition soon began to seep through to the interior of the flat, and by midsummer Nilsen was spraying air fresheners and disinfectants about the place. These, however, did little to ameliorate the situation and Nilsen was forced to exhume the bodies. He dissected them, putting the heads into plastic rubbish bags and the torsos into two suitcases which he stored in a shed at the bottom of the garden to which he had a key. Arms and hands were buried in the garden, and viscera were dumped in plastic bags by the dustbins for the refuse collectors to remove. A passer-by found one of these, however, before the dustmen arrived. He took it to the police, saying it looked suspiciously like human internal organs. The police dismissed the idea and said it was simply butcher's refuse.

In the late summer of that same year – probably between July and September – Nilsen went on a pub-crawl in the West End with a 26-year-old Scot named Billy Sutherland. Predictably, they ended up in Nilsen's flat, where the Scot was strangled with a tie. Nilsen left him sitting in an armchair for two days before the usual ritual of washing in the bath, changing underwear and fondling the body. Sutherland's last resting place was where the bodies of his two predecessors had lain prior to their dismemberment – beneath the floorboards.

Victim number five, picked up in the Salisbury at the end of the year, could have been either a Filipino or a Latin American according to Nilsen, but his origin was never ascertained. The sixth victim was an Irish builders' labourer, inveigled to the death flat from the Cricklewood Arms. The seventh was an emaciated, ill-nourished young dosser whom Nilsen had found huddled in a shop doorway at the end of Oxford Street where it adjoins Charing Cross Road. Nilsen took him home and gave him a meal, and they drank a bottle of rum between them. When the young man was in a drunken stupor, Nilsen strangled him with a tie. He was so thin and wasted – 'he looked just like a Belsen victim' – that Nilsen could not bear to look at his naked body but bundled him unceremoniously into a plastic bag and burned him in the garden as soon as he could.

Nilsen could remember little about the eighth victim,

beyond saying that he had put the body under the floor, taken it out and dismembered it into three sections, and then replaced it under the floorboards. Victims nine and ten were both Scots. Both were eighteen, and both had been picked up in the Golden Lion in Dean Street. They eventually joined their comrades in death beneath the by now overcrowded space under the floor of the flat.

By the end of the year Nilsen thought it was high time, to coin a phrase, to get rid of the plethora of bodies – 'wall to wall bodies', as he later described them. He built another bonfire in the garden – a huge one which attracted a number of neighbourhood children – and set to dismembering the remains and burning them in the usual black plastic refuse bag shroud, heaping car tyres on top. A vast quantity of tyres went up in acrid smoke, keeping the bonfire burning all day. When the funeral pyre had burned itself out, Nilsen got busy with a lawn roller and crushed the remaining bone fragments to powder. Then he raked over the site. Neighbours may well have thought he was a keen gardener as he went about his grisly task, but none of them had the slightest inkling of the grim reality that lay behind his apparent industry.

Having disposed of his 'problem', as he dubbed it, Nilsen had no intention of halting his murderous spree. To celebrate his relief at having at last rid himself of the incriminating and malodorous bodies, he went out the same night to a pub and bringing a young man home for sex decided on a whim to let him live. He left the next morning unharmed.

Reverting to his true form, Nilsen picked up his eleventh victim in Leicester Square. This was a Cockney skinhead who had a row of dots tattooed around his neck superimposed by the inscription 'Cut along dotted line'. When Nilsen dissected his body, he did just that. He became the first of the next group to occupy the under-floor space.

Malcolm Barlow, aged twenty-four, was in the wrong place at the wrong time. Nilsen found him literally on his doorstep, sitting slumped against a wall in Melrose Avenue, only yards from the death flat. He was an epileptic and had suffered from a fit in the street, after which someone had propped him up. Nilsen, however, did not immediately seize the unemployed vagrant from Yorkshire and take him into his flat; instead he called an ambulance, which took Barlow to hospital.

The following day he discharged himself from hospital, against medical advice, and went to look for the Good Samaritan who had helped him. He found the house in which Nilsen lived, and sat on the front steps to wait for him to come home from work at about six o'clock. He invited himself in, and asked Nilsen for a drink. Nilsen had misgivings about this because he knew that the young chap took medication for his epilepsy. He warned Barlow that alcohol and his tablets might not mix. Barlow said he was willing to risk it. Nilsen cooked him a meal and they drank a quantity of rum; Barlow quickly became unconscious. Nilsen strangled him, and he was laid to rest beside the Cockney skinhead with the grotesque tattoo.

Barlow was the last man to die in the Melrose Avenue charnel house. Nilsen's landlord had been offered a very substantial sum for the house by property developers, one of the conditions being that it was to be purchased with vacant possession. The landlord then set about offering all the tenants cash settlements to induce them to leave. He offered Nilsen one thousand pounds, which he accepted, and started looking for a larger flat to move into. Finding one to his liking, he took the tenancy, but there was one snag: it had no garden. There would be no bonfires to burn his victims, and he would have to devise some other method of disposal of the bodies. Before moving, of course, he would also have to have one final funeral pyre to dispose of the bodies he already had under the floor and also, dismembered in plastic bags, in the garden shed. This he did, and on 5 October 1981 he moved to his new flat at 23 Cranleigh Gardens, Muswell Hill, with his little dog named Bleep. For a time, he busied himself with decorating his new flat and arranging his furniture and belongings to his liking, as well as stocking up with booze. He would certainly be inviting young men to his new abode, though he would have nowhere to cremate them. That was the problem which led to his undoing.

In March 1982 Nilsen met John Howlett, known to all and sundry as 'John the Guardsman', although actually he had never been in the Guards but was a 23-year-old unemployed drifter from High Wycombe in Buckinghamshire. Although Nilsen had willingly invited him back to the flat for drinks, he became annoyed when Howlett made himself, to use Nilsen's words, 'too much at home'. 'I didn't know you were moving in,' said Nilsen sarcastically. 'I think it's time you went, so you'd better go.' Howlett had become so drunk that he was practically comatose, and while in this state Nilsen throttled him with his bare hands until he lost consciousness completely, then drowned him in the bath.

The floorboards in Nilsen's new flat were impossible to lift unless he had been prepared to use tools and make a considerable amount of noise, which would have attracted the attention of other tenants. So he dissected the body, boiled the head in a large cooking pot, put the largest of the bones out with the rubbish for the dustmen, and the flesh of the torso, arms and legs into a tea chest which stood in one of his rooms. He then flushed the internal organs and some small portions of flesh down the toilet.

Nilsen's fourteenth victim was Graham Allan, a Glaswegian of twenty-eight years who was a drug addict and alcoholic. Nilsen cooked him a meal, during which Allan fell asleep, since he was already drunk when Nilsen took him home. In his later statement Nilsen says that he has no recollection of killing the man, but that he 'found him to be dead'. He removed his clothes and washed his body in the bath, where he was left for two days. Then he was subjected to the same treatment as the previous victim.

Nilsen's last victim was another drug addict whom he found in The George public house in Goslett's Yard on 1 February 1983. He did not know it, but eight days later he would be arrested. The man, Stephen Sinclair, twenty, had a prison record and suffered from hepatitis. They spent the evening watching TV and listening to rock music, drinking whisky and beer; Sinclair also injected himself with drugs.

Once again Nilsen, according to his statement, had no memory of killing Sinclair; he said that he was so drunk that he could not remember anything of what happened. The body was left in the bedroom for a couple of days, covered by a blanket. When Nilsen had sobered up sufficiently, he cut off the head and set it to boil in the large pot, while he went out to the pub with Bleep, his small dog. He cut up the body and bagged it, but subsequently decided that he would have to get rid of it, so he put the largest portions out with the rubbish and flushed smaller parts down the toilet. Nemesis was creeping nearer and nearer …

The tea chest with its grisly contents was becoming more and more odoriferous. The boiled heads of the last two victims were bagged and put into the wardrobe along with other bagged remains that had already been placed there, and Nilsen shut the door on them. He then considered what he should do to get rid of the remains in the tea chest. To this end, he removed the complete lower half of a torso and left it in the bathroom in preparation for a dissection job which would enable him to bag the remains in smaller portions and take them out to the dustbins; he had no compunction about using other people's dustbins when his own became full.

Spraying more disinfectant and air freshener around the flat, he finally flushed the last of the smaller remains –

hands, fingers, internal organs – down the toilet. And it was not long after this that the other tenants started complaining to the landlord about the blocked drains, saying that their toilets were clogged up and unflushable. As we have seen, things came to a head the following Tuesday, 8 February – the day that Nilsen finally met his Waterloo.

The day before his arrest, Nilsen had appeared perfectly normal at the Jobcentre where he worked. Nobody noticed the slightest trace of nervous tension or other unusual behaviour. It was the same calm, emotionless façade that was to see him right through all his interrogations and his subsequent trial.

The pathologist who examined the remains found in the flat discovered that the two large black plastic bin liners contained a series of smaller plastic carrier bags. One contained a male left thoracic segment including the arm still attached; in another was a torso with all limbs removed. A third contained lungs, heart, spleen, liver, gall bladder, kidneys and intestines. The dissection had been carried out with some degree of skill, the doctor was able to say. Nilsen evidently had a good knowledge of human anatomy. The pathologist was able to match up the lower torso that had been found in the bathroom to upper body parts found in the tea chest. The three victims from the Cranleigh Gardens flat were identified variously from dental records, fingerprints, blood grouping and, in one case, the distinctive fracture of the jaw the man had sustained in a fight, which showed up on a skull X-ray. If DNA printing had been in use at that time the pathologist's task would have been made immeasurably easier.

The questioning lasted a week, during which Nilsen gave the police officers a precise and detailed account of all the murders, bar the two he could not remember killing owing to his drunken state at the time. He told DCI Peter

Jay, 'It's a good job you've arrested me now. If you'd waited till I was sixty-five, there'd have been thousands of bodies to look through.' The interviewing officers could barely conceal their revulsion.

Nilsen had a bizarre sense of humour. During his interrogation he asked for an ashtray to stub out the cigarette he'd smoked, and when a young constable told him to flush it down the toilet, Nilsen replied, 'The last time I flushed something down the toilet I got into real trouble.'

Asked whether the murders had been premeditated, Nilsen told his interrogators that he did not go out looking for victims with the intent of killing them once he had lured them back to his flat. 'The killings just happened,' Nilsen said. He added that a far greater number of young men had left his flat alive than had been killed. But he said that he felt no remorse, and could not feel anything at all for his victims. 'Inside me,' he said, 'I was just completely cold and devoid of feeling.'

Later Nilsen's solicitor asked him to try to explain to him why he had killed the men. He said he had no explanation. 'Maybe someone else may be able to tell me why I did what I did,' he said quizzically.

Nilsen was remanded to Brixton Prison, where he saw the tabloid headlines such as 'The House of Horrors' and became very conscious of media interest in his case. At last he had become a 'somebody' – at last he had won the recognition he craved, albeit via the notoriety of crime of the most heinous and repellent nature.

The trial began on Monday, 24 October 1983, at the Old Bailey before Mr Justice Croom-Johnson. Prosecuting was Mr Alan Green, QC, and Mr Ivan Lawrence, QC, defended the accused, who was charged with six murders and two attempted murders. He had actually confessed to fifteen murders and seven attempted ones. He pleaded not guilty to murder but guilty of manslaughter on the grounds of diminished responsibility.

The prosecution outlined the facts of the case to the eight-man, four-woman jury. He said that seven of the victims had been positively identified, although only six were named in the indictment. Mr Green pointed out the pattern of the murders: all the victims were young men, all but one had been picked up in pubs, and all were complete strangers to the accused. With one exception, all were drifters or vagrants of no fixed abode. Some of them, though not all, were homosexuals, as was Nilsen himself. It had been forensically proved that Nilsen had sexual relations with six of the bodies.

Mr Green read Nilsen's confession to the shocked and horror-stricken court. When the police had asked him how many bodies he had in his flat at any one time, Mr Green said, Nilsen had replied, 'I'm not sure. I did not do a stock check.'

The first witnesses called by the prosecution were various men who had escaped with their lives (some barely) after Nilsen's murderous attacks. The police had been aware of these attacks only after Nilsen had confessed to them in his long and detailed statement. The survivors came forward to testify only at the request of the police; originally they had not wished to press charges as they did not wish to be publicly branded as homosexuals. Detective Inspector Chambers gave evidence that he had been able to trace fourteen young men who had visited Nilsen's flat and come to no harm.

On the third day of the trial Mr Lawrence, for the defence, told the jury that he was not attempting to prove that Nilsen was insane, but that at the time of the murders he had been suffering from an abnormality of mind. He called Dr James McKeith, a psychiatrist, as his first witness.

The doctor averred that Nilsen suffered from a severe personality defect and that at the times of the killings he was suffering from a condition known as 'disassociation', which could be most easily described as a person feeling that he was actually watching someone else perform the action in question. Under cross-examination by the prosecution the doctor had to admit that a psychiatrist's knowledge of a person's mental state was limited to what he could evaluate from that person's own statements. Mr Green was at pains to point out that if Nilsen could desist from killing in some cases, then that showed that he had the power of choice, which was proof of rational thinking and ruled out 'temporary insanity'.

Nilsen was quoted as having said that he was a 'creative psychopath' who became a 'destructive psychopath' under the influence of alcohol. There was certainly no doubt that he was an alcoholic, but it was a controlled kind of alcoholism, in that he managed to abstain during the day in order to be sober enough to carry out his duties at work and so keep his job. But at night, after work, his alcoholism was allowed to take over and distort his entire personality, with the results that caused him to end up in the dock on a multiple murder charge. Proof enough, if such were needed, the psychiatrist continued, that Nilsen's responsibility was indeed diminished and that he was a victim like the men he had killed, though in a different sense.

The prosecution disagreed, pointing out that the decision to remain sober by day to avoid losing his job, but to give rein to his craving for alcohol after working hours, was, again, a matter which proved free choice and thus, *ipso facto*, that he was capable of rational thinking.

Another psychiatrist put up as a witness stated that Nilsen could not have had 'malice aforethought' to commit the murders if as he had himself stated he had no feelings. At this point the judge rebuked the witness and told him not to trespass in the realms of the law but to confine himself to medical opinions.

The prosecution insisted that free choice formed an

integral part of Nilsen's behaviour; he chose to invite men to his flat, he chose to go out looking for them. He chose to murder Malcolm Barlow because, according to his own confession, the man had 'become a nuisance'. In his closing speech Mr Green said, 'When all is said and done, you are dealing here with a man who enjoyed killing people and derived satisfaction from the act of killing. The defence says that this man was simply out of his mind and couldn't help it. The Crown says, oh yes, he could!'

The judge's summing-up took four hours, and some people felt that he was somewhat biased against the defendant and sceptical of the claims of psychiatrists. 'There are evil people who do evil things,' he declared, 'and committing repeated acts of murder is one of them.'

The jury retired to consider their verdict on the morning of Thursday 3 November, and at 4.30 p.m. the judge asked them whether they had been able to reach a decision. They had not, and the judge ordered them to be sequestered in a hotel overnight. At ten o'clock the next morning they returned to the jury room to resume their deliberations. The judge informed them that he would be prepared to accept a majority verdict, and at 4.25 p.m. they returned to the courtroom ready to announce their decision.

The foreman of the jury announced that there was a majority verdict of ten to two of guilty of murder on all counts. And on all the counts of attempted murder, they had voted ten to two for guilty except for one of the indictments under this heading, when their verdict had been unanimous.

On Friday 4 November 1983, after the ten-day trial with all its sensational revelations of horror, Dennis Nilsen was sentenced to life imprisonment, with the proviso that he should serve a minimum of twenty-five years.

9

The Misbegotten

Albert Fish (1928)

The famous German psychiatrist Karl Berg, in his definitive study of Peter Kürten, the Düsseldorf Monster, called Kürten 'the king of sexual delinquents'. Despite the fact that the subject of this chapter, Albert Hamilton Fish, was contemporaneous with Kürten, Berg made no pronouncements on Fish. This may be purely because Fish was an American, while Berg's field of operation was Germany, but if Berg had been able to examine Fish in the same manner that he interviewed Kürten, without a shadow of doubt he would have relegated Kürten to second place and nominated Fish as the prime contender for this title.

There is no known practice in the annals of sexual deviation that was not espoused by Albert Hamilton Fish. Some of the things he did are not even mentioned in Krafft-Ebing.

As is so often the case with serial murderers, psychopaths and psychotics, Fish was a mild-looking, inoffensive little man whom nobody would ever have associated with crime of any kind, let alone crimes of the most horrendous kind. Fish was not only a sado-masochist and a serial murderer but also a self-confessed child molester, cannibal and coprophagic necrophile to boot.

Dr Fredric Wertham, a psychiatrist who testified at the later trial, discovered that Fish had not just one but no fewer than seven 'skeletons in the family closet'. His mother was considered to be 'a bit queer' by her neighbours and friends, who said that she 'heard voices' inaudible to others, and 'saw things' that were not there. His father was seventy-five at the time the boy was born, and died when the young Albert was five years old. An uncle on his father's side was psychotic and suffered from hallucinations, and a half-brother was committed to a state asylum for the insane. A younger brother died at an early age of hydrocephalus ('water on the brain'), while one of his sisters was epileptic. Another sister died young in an institution, though the record does not specify what kind.

When his father died, the 5-year-old Albert was sent to St John's Orphanage in Washington, DC, where he received a very thorough grounding in sado-masochism at the hands of the brutal staff, who used to strip boys naked and beat them on their bare bottoms for the slightest misdemeanours. Dr Wertham in his testimony pointed out that it was at this stage that Albert learned to associate pain with pleasure. Before the age of seven the boy experienced his first sexual feelings, which he had discovered were aroused, first by seeing other boys whipped, then by being whipped himself. In addition, the boy was a bed-wetter until he was eleven years of age, and he was described as being a 'very highly strung and nervous' type of boy. Academically, he was average.

On leaving the school Albert decided to take up the trade of house painter and decorator. This was not merely an obvious choice for a young man without higher academic qualifications or further education beyond the tenth grade. As a paedophile, he could easily obtain work in schools, children's hospitals, YMCAs and boys' clubs and other places where there would be young boys. Also, by adopting the practice of wearing his painter's overalls only and no other clothing except socks and shoes, he could strip quickly for his nefarious activities and then as quickly dress again afterwards and disappear from the scene. Carrying his cans of paint, brushes and sometimes a ladder, he could depart from a building at a leisurely pace without calling attention to himself. No one would pay any attention to him, nor remember him later when the body of a raped and murdered victim was later found in the building, or the screams of a child brought someone rushing to the scene.

His sexual preferences were for young boys between four or five and fourteen or so, but he was certainly not averse to girls in the same age-group. Being bisexual, he would sometimes take a man or a woman as a sexual partner, but only if he could not find a younger victim – he did not kill or maim adults. He married one wife legally and three bigamously without being apprehended by the law, but he did attempt to choose as partners women who were at least agreeable to indulge in sado-masochistic and other perversions with him, even if they were not wildly enthusiastic. In fact all his wives left him when it all got a bit too much to cope with.

Even without the bizarre sexual aberrations, Fish's behaviour must have frightened some of his wives out of their wits. For example, he had a habit of going out into the garden, beating his breast and screaming 'I am Christ!' at the top of his voice, even in broad daylight with the neighbours looking on, as well as at night when they would more likely bang on the wall telling him in no uncertain terms to stop the noise as they were trying to sleep. Then what were the wives to think of a husband who took roses from the garden and inserted them (complete with thorns) into his penis while looking at himself in the mirror, after which he would eat the flowers? Even Krafft-Ebing had never heard of that one.

By the time of the trial, police were able to link Fish to rapes and murders in no fewer than twenty-three states, but Fish himself stated that he had claimed victims in every state in the Union, and estimated the number of children he had raped or murdered to be something around 400 between 1910 and 1934, although the police could link him positively to only one hundred crimes. Like many of these perverts, including Peter Kürten before him, he was obsessed with telling the truth about his exploits, complete with all the gory details, and there is no reason to suppose he was lying. He had nothing to lose, so there would have been no point in bragging that he had committed more outrages than had actually occurred.

Fish travelled around America, sometimes losing a job contract because of being suspected of child abuse, when he would hastily pack up and go, thus avoiding being arrested on suspicion. He was so ordinary looking, so nondescript, that it was literally impossible to trace him. One feature of his attacks was that he rendered himself more vulnerable to discovery because he did not gag his victims as he liked to hear them scream. Therefore, he did not kill them if they were in an isolated location, only if the proximity of other people might arouse suspicion when they heard the agonized screaming of young victims of the assaults. There were, of course, a number of exceptions such as when he intended killing the victim anyway for the satisfaction of his cannibalistic urges.

By the time he was fifty, in 1920, Fish was already well advanced into cannibalism and would habitually dismember the bodies of his victims and remove strips of flesh, visceral organs and other parts and cook them. To quote his own words, 'consuming these tender morsels gave me much greater sexual pleasure than actual sexual activities with the bodies'. By this time in his life, he was already far along the paths of extreme perversion, including coprophagy, as well as the drinking of urine and the drinking of blood, including his own. Another of his bizarre perversions was to insert needles into his pelvic area, some so deeply that they could not be removed; an X-ray taken in prison showed twenty-nine needles in his body, some eroded by time into fragments. He would also push balls of cotton wool soaked in methylated spirits or other alcohol into his rectum and set them alight, or push a lighted cigarette into his anus. There were occasions when his children from his first marriage would ask him what he was doing when they entered his bedroom and found him beating himself on the bare buttocks. He would then induce the children to carry on belabouring him with paddles 'because it is easier for someone else to do it than to do it oneself'. It would be easy to assume that his first wife discovered them in such a situation and precipitately took the children and left him, though this is pure speculation.

It was at about this time, too, that Fish's religious fervour reached a peak of obsession. He began to hallucinate that he had visions in which God had ordered him to castrate and kill young boys – which he promptly did. It is amazing that during these years of madness he was never caught. Boys simply disappeared and were never seen again. Widespread speculation at the time of the trial avers that the tender parts of the bodies were cooked and eaten and the bones and other remains buried in remote locations.

One boy, however, had a fortunate escape and was able to testify some years later that after meeting Fish and allowing himself to be tied up (Fish had said 'it's just a game'). Fish had whipped him until his buttocks bled and then attempted unsuccessfully to cut off his genitals with a pair of scissors. Fish panicked and fled when the boy screamed. A motorist heard the boy's agonized cries and took him to the hospital. Unfortunately the boy was unable to describe his attacker beyond saying that he was 'a short man', white and middle-aged.

Fish spent much of his time seeking out passages in the Bible which appealed to his state of mind, such as the story of Abraham sacrificing his son Isaac. He felt that God wished him to sacrifice a young boy in similar fashion. It is not known how many boys were 'sacrificed' in this way, but between 1911 and the trial twenty-three years later a number of boys aged between four and fifteen disappeared in locations where Fish was known to be at the material time and were never seen again. One is tempted to say, with a good deal of justification, that the police were falling down on the job, and that if these outrages had been taking place in this day and age it would not have taken them twenty-three years to find him. This is particularly so with the case about to be described – the case that finally brought this misbegotten monster to justice.

On Sunday, 27 May 1928, a teenage boy sat reading the *New York World* at his home, 406 West Fifteenth Street, in Manhattan. He was checking to see that an advertisement he had placed in the paper a few days previously had appeared. It read: 'Young man, 18, wishes position in country. Edward Budd, 406 West Fifteenth Street ...'

Someone else, too, was reading the *New York World* that Sunday: Albert Hamilton Fish, in another part of New York City. He spotted Edward Budd's advertisement. Eighteen was a bit old for a boy to his liking, but you never know, so many of these older teenagers never looked anything like their age. One young chap he had taken for fourteen, had in fact, it turned out, been a very under-developed 19-year-old, and mentally retarded to boot. Still, Fish was not one to pass up an opportunity. He did not, of course, intend to offer Edward Budd, or anyone else, employment of any kind, and if the young chap was not his type, he would concoct some excuse and leave.

His knock at the door of number 406 was answered by Mrs Delia Budd, a large woman in her early forties; the large-flowered print overall she was wearing made her look even bigger. 'What can I do for you?' she said to the kindly looking little old man standing on her doorstep.

Fish looked up at the formidable Mrs Budd with his watery blue eyes. 'I've come about this advertisement,' he said, pointing to Edward Budd's classified 'ad' in the paper he carried folded to the appropriate page. 'My name is Frank Howard. I have an offer of a job that may interest your son. I assume Edward *is* your son?'

'He most certainly is,' the woman replied. 'Come in, please, Mr Howard, and make yourself at home. Ted isn't in at the moment, but I can easily get him for you. He's only round at his friend's.' She called to one of her younger children. 'Beatrice! Go round to Tom's place and tell Ted to come home straightaway. Tell him a gentleman has come to see him about that job ad he put in the paper.'

Some gentleman! But Mrs Budd was not to know what kind of a fiend she had invited into her home.

The 5-year-old Beatrice nipped next door-but-three and returned with her brother. Meanwhile Mrs Budd removed a pile of folded clean laundry from the old, shabby sofa so that 'Mr Howard' could take a seat. While Mrs Budd was preparing tea and home-made gingerbread biscuits, 'Mr Howard' regaled Edward with tales from his fertile imagination of his farm on Long Island, the three hundred chickens and the half-dozen milking cows – not to mention the five farmhands he employed (including a milkmaid) and a cook. The script would have done credit to a 'B' movie.

From Fish's point of view, Edward was a non-runner from the word go. Powerfully built, he looked more like a man of twenty-two or twenty-three than a youth of eighteen. Not his type at all. After settling on the wages for the non-existent farm job – fifteen dollars a week – Fish knew that he would have to do some fast thinking to get out of that one. A two-room apartment in the Bronx was hardly big enough for one chicken, let alone three hundred. And where would he put those cows? Meanwhile, Mrs Budd was beaming huge smiles of satisfaction all over her face as her son conducted the negotiations with the affable stranger.

'I will come for you next Sunday,' 'Mr Howard' told Edward, 'and take you to my farm.' That would give him a week to think up some plausible excuse. But he *would* return to the house; he had spotted a slender child playing outside the house, and was determined to ascertain this very attractive child's identity.

The following Sunday, true to his word and carrying a pail of pot cheese and a basket of strawberries, he knocked once again at the Budd family's door. Handing the cheese and the strawberries to Mr and Mrs Budd as a gift 'from his farm' (he had actually purchased both items from street vendors on his way to the house), he observed that Edward had a duffel bag ready packed with his spare clothes and other items in anticipation of the forthcoming job. Mr and Mrs Budd invited their guest to stay to lunch, which he did.

Scarcely able to mask his excitement, Fish discovered that the slender child he had seen the previous week was in fact one of the Budds' children. Dressed in knockabout play overalls, Fish had taken the child for a boy. Now, however, he saw that it was a girl, wearing the white dress, white socks and black patent shoes she habitually wore to attend church, from which she had just returned home. A girl! – but still slender and unformed, with a boyish, prepubertal figure. Slender – and doubtless tender … The loathsome predator's mind was made up. But first he had to dispose of the problem of Edward and the 'farm job'.

'I'm very sorry, Ted,' he told the youth as they sat at table, 'I'm afraid the job will not be able to start for another week. The man you will be replacing needs another week to find a new living-in farm job. So I'm afraid you'll have to hang on for another week. I'll come and pick you up next Sunday.' It was easy to see the disappointment in the youth's face. His father tried to comfort him, 'A week's only seven days, lad,' he said. 'It'll soon go.'

'Say hi to Mr Howard, Grace,' said Mrs Budd as the slender 10-year-old came up to the chair which had been placed for her beside the stranger. Shyly she did. Fish put an arm round her shoulders and fished in a pocket for some loose change. 'There you are, my dear,' he said, placing fifty cents in her hand. 'Treat yourself to some candy after lunch.' The child was so flabbergasted at this unexpected and unaccustomed largesse that she had to be prompted by her mother to thank their visitor. Treats were few and far between in this very poor working-class family.

Fish took the child on his lap, holding her there with one arm while ostensibly fishing for more coins in his pocket. After what seemed an unconscionable length of time, he eventually produced a quarter for Beatrice, and two dollar bills which he handed to Edward. 'You and Tom go to the movies tonight,' he said.

The stolid Mr Budd, who never talked much anyway, was lost for words, while his wife blushed furiously as she stuttered her thanks.

'You really ought not to … ' The simple, unpretentious couple were clearly impressed by the stranger's generosity, but unfortunately not astute or sophisticated enough to see through the unscrupulous ploy of an evil man ingratiating himself with them for some nefarious purpose of his own.

'I had a letter from my sister a few days ago,' Fish said between bites of sauerkraut and *bockwurst*, 'saying she's having a party for my niece's eighth birthday. Would you let me take Grace there? She'd enjoy it. There would be about ten little girls and boys there. I'd bring her back by nine o'clock sharp. What do you say?'

Mr and Mrs Budd looked at one another without speaking. Would it be okay to let the child go? She had so little opportunities for enjoyment. But we hardly know the fellow. The unspoken query hung between them; they could scarcely discuss it in their guest's presence. Grace was a quiet and obedient child; she did not venture a word, but the exciting prospect of the entertainment was clearly visible in her eyes.

It was Mr Budd who broke the silence. 'Let the kid go,' he said. 'She doesn't get out much except to go to school and to church. Where is the place?'

'It's on 137th Street and Columbus Avenue. A really nice building. In a nice area, too.'

Mrs Budd helped Grace into her best Sunday coat with its fur-trimmed collar and cuffs, and a matching grey velvet bonnet with blue streamers. An imitation rose was pinned to her lapel, and she carried a little blue beaded bag. Trustfully clutching her new friend's hand, she said good-bye to her parents, brother and his friend Tom, and sister Beatrice, who sat contentedly on the rug munching candy from a paper bag. Mrs Budd followed the pair out and watched them from the front stoop of their apartment building as they made their way to the corner, turned right and were lost to sight. Little did the mother know that she would never see the child again.

* * *

At nine o'clock there was no sign of 'Mr Howard' and Grace, but Mr and Mrs Budd decided to give them a bit longer to allow for such possibilities as late buses. But when ten o'clock came and went and there was still no sign of them, they became concerned and Mr Budd went to the police station on Twentieth Street to report his daughter missing and give them a description of the stranger to whom they had so foolishly entrusted her.

A short time later Police Lieutenant Samuel Dribben, with three detectives, called at their home to question the frantic couple more closely about the 'gentleman farmer' who had twenty acres at Farmingdale on Long Island, Frank Howard, aged probably in his late fifties or early sixties, who had purportedly taken Grace to his niece's birthday party at an apartment on 137th Street and Columbus Avenue and promised to return her by nine o'clock.

Lieutenant Dribben looked at his three detectives, and they looked knowingly back at him. Columbus Avenue ends at 110th Street, they pointed out. There is no 137th Street. The plausible old man had given them an address that did not exist.

Delia Budd and her husband had lived all their lives in Manhattan, but like many working-class people of that time they rarely ventured out of their immediate neighbourhood and were quite unaware of the geography of New York's sprawling intersection system.

By now the couple's initial panic had subsided into a kind of resigned stupor, as they realized that there was nothing they could do but hope the police could eventually trace their child, hopefully unharmed, and the man who had taken her. The police knew that it could not be a kidnap for ransom, since the family lived in poverty, barely above the breadline. The husband was employed as a mechanic, and Edward, the eldest son, was actively seeking a job. Mrs Budd took in sewing if she could get it.

Dribben's first move was to check whether there was a farmer named Howard who had a spread in Farmingdale,

Long Island. The policeman was not at all surprised to ascertain that no such person had a smallholding of any kind in the vicinity. Nor was he able to turn up any elderly man in the area to match the description the Budds had been able to give him. Next he took Edward, the eldest son, to the police station to look through the albums of 'mug shots' of known criminals to see if any of the faces looked anything like that of the abductor of his sister. Edward was unable to recognize him among them. It seemed on the face of it, therefore, that he had no previous 'form', at least in New York City.

Detectives Jerry Maher and James McGee were detailed to make a thorough door-to-door search of the dozens of shabby rooming-houses in the area to see if the man was local. They came up empty-handed. The detectives then turned their attention to empty lots, back alleys, cellars and crawl spaces under buildings, subways, derelict buildings, even rooftops. But no trace of the missing girl could be found. It was a gloomy Lieutenant Dribben who presided at a conference: what to do next?

Predictably, the tabloids were quick to take up the challenge to their readers to help find the innocent and trusting girl who had walked out of her home on a sunny Sunday afternoon, with her parents' permission, clutching the hand of a kindly looking old man who had promised to take her to a birthday party and bring her back by nine o'clock. Had she been lured to an unknown fate by a fiend in the guise of a friendly grandfather figure – a ravening wolf in the clothing of a lamb? The tabloids seemed to think so – and so, of course, did the police, though they were much less vociferous about it. After all, they did not want to upset the Budds, who were clinging desperately to the hope that there was some innocuous explanation and that Grace would soon be restored to the bosom of her family. Nor did they want to panic the population into thinking that there was a child murderer loose on the streets.

Predictably, both the newspapers and the police were swamped with calls reporting 'little old men' loitering about and staring at their children, hanging about school playgrounds and parks, and so on. Police pointed out that it was not a crime to look at somebody, but they could only take any action if children were accosted or molested in any way. Several calls did report attempted abductions, but the children came to no harm, running off home. When a woman reported that an elderly man had tried to lure her 10-year-old son into the hallway of a tenement building, police quickly arrived and arrested a 59-year-old carpenter. He admitted having approached the boy, but denied harming him. He looked nothing like the elusive 'Frank Howard' and had no knowledge of the abduction of Grace Budd. He was discharged with a caution.

On the Thursday (7 June) a thousand flyers were printed with a photograph of Grace Budd and a description of the child and of 'Frank Howard' and distributed to police departments throughout the United States and Canada. Later several thousand more copies were produced and posted up in New York City's subways, post offices, banks, department stores, corner shops, barber shops, kosher butchers, lunch counters, restaurants – every possible location to catch the public eye. No stone would be left unturned.

The result of this massive saturation was a flood of false sightings. 'Mr Howard' was spotted in twenty or thirty places – many simultaneously – in five of the north-eastern states. Some of these alleged sightings placed him as far away as Niagara Falls and across the border. Some said the man was alone, while others averred that he had a little girl in tow. All these reports were checked and led nowhere. A grandfather of short stature could scarcely go out for a walk with his granddaughter, especially in New York City, without being stopped by the cops.

One slender clue surfaced: Detective McGee managed

to locate the street vendor who had sold the pail of pot cheese and the basket of strawberries that Fish had purchased and given to the Budds. The vendor, Reuben Rosoff, who peddled his wares from a pushcart on 100th Street at Second Avenue, was able to identify the hand-inscribed price of 40c on the bottom of the pail as his own writing. He was also able to give the police a very good description of his customer, having noted particular characteristics such as the watery-looking blue eyes, the wispy gray moustache and the very soft voice, and the fact that he was not more than 5 ft. 5 in. in height. All these points tallied exactly with the description given by the Budds. And Rosoff said that the man was certainly no farmer, gentleman or otherwise.

No more leads were forthcoming, and the case gradually wound down in prominence in the New York newspapers. Other more pressing news, both national and international, crowded out the Budd case. But in their zeal to arrest a suspect, the police, who were of course still hunting the elusive kidnapper, apprehended no fewer than three men and got them as far as court before it became palpably evident that none of them could possibly have had any connection with the abduction of Grace Budd. One of these men, indeed, had been fingered by his wife, who was so fed up with her errant husband that she accused him in the hope that he would be sent to jail out of her way!

To attempt to break this impasse, late in the summer of 1928 the investigation was put under the command of Lieutenant William F. King, who was transferred from the Missing Persons Bureau owing to his many years' expertise in hunting out those who had disappeared, whether victims or suspected criminals. Gradually, as he familiarized himself with the details of the Budd case, King became completely absorbed – indeed, to quote his own words, obsessed with his objective: to find Grace

Budd, alive or dead, at all costs and to bring to justice the shadowy figure who was responsible for her disappearance. In his own mind, as an experienced police veteran well-versed in such matters as well as a gut feeling, King was convinced that the girl had met a violent end at the hands of a child killer motivated by lust. Just how hideous the crime was, and how depraved the man who had committed it, would not become clear for some considerable time yet. But King vowed to be there when the time came.

* * *

On 15 December 1930 a withered-looking old man with watery blue eyes and a drooping gray moustache was arrested and committed to Bellevue Hospital psychiatric ward in New York City for a ten-day observation period. He had been arrested for sending obscene mail through the postal system. The specific charge read that he had sent 'a letter of such a vile, obscene and filthy nature that the contents thereof would defile the court records'. Having seen a transcript of this letter, I cannot but agree: its contents were far too disgusting for me to reproduce them in this book.

The man, it appeared, was a compulsive writer of obscene letters to complete strangers, obtaining women's names and addresses from various sources, including directories, newspaper advertisements and the so-called 'lonely hearts' columns. He had embarked on this course early in 1929. Now the recipient of his latest scatological outpourings was so horrified that she handed the letter immediately to the police.

The man had conducted his depraved correspondence under a number of aliases and fictitious addresses and box numbers, but gave the police who arrested him his real name: Albert Hamilton Fish.

In the hospital, Fish was interviewed by a psychiatrist who in turn presented his findings to the head of the hospital's psychiatric department, Dr M.S. Gregory. During the ten-day observation period, Gregory's notes stated, Fish had been 'quiet and co-operative' and had conducted himself in 'an orderly and normal manner'. There had been no evidence of hallucinations, hearing voices or other delusions. It was true that the subject showed some of the degenerative changes associated with senility, but his memory and mental capacity were excellent for his age of sixty years.

However, Gregory qualified his report by stating that the subject certainly had a sexual psychopathy in his mental makeup, as abundantly proved by the contents of the letter, but that, to quote Gregory's own words, 'did not mean that he was insane or a danger to others'. There would come the day when Gregory would eat his words, but that was some years ahead yet. Fish looked so harmless, just a decrepit old man, that it was almost impossible for even experienced doctors to judge the depths of depravity embodied in that frail-looking frame. Gregory was not the first, nor would he be the last, to be wildly off the mark with his diagnosis. Fish – like many other criminals – was as cunning as a fox at concealing his true nature under a thin veneer of pseudo-normality when it suited his purposes.

Fish was kept on the ward in Bellevue Hospital for thirty days – almost three weeks longer than the original ten-day observation order. At the end of that time, Gregory and his colleagues saw no reason to amend their original conclusions, and the report was routinely passed on to Judge Frank J. Coleman, of the US District Court for the southern section of New York City. On 16 January Fish was discharged from the hospital into the custody of his eldest married daughter, Mrs Anna Collins of Astoria, Queens, to whom Fish had written from hospital asking her to apply for his release. The judge placed him on probation, and Fish was let loose to roam the streets and continue with his horrendous peregrinations.

Fish did not stay long with his daughter. He had so many weird habits that she was seriously concerned at the effect some of them might have on her impressionable young children. So she asked her father to move out. He found an apartment of four rooms at 1883 Amsterdam Avenue, on Manhattan's Upper West Side, and invited his younger unmarried son, also named Albert, to share with him. They were very shortly afterwards invited by the superintendent of the block to become joint maintenance managers for the three apartment buildings which made up the block. They readily agreed, Albert jun. doing the painting and decorating, carpentry and plumbing repairs, while his father did the lighter chores and on occasion collected the tenants' rents in the superintendent's absence. Both Fish and his son were, according to the superintendent's later evidence, exemplary employees and no complaint of any kind was ever made about their work.

The same could not be said, however, about Fish's behaviour. One afternoon during the summer of 1931 the 35-year-old Albert jun. was repainting the lobby of Number 1887 when a tenant came looking for him to report a burst pipe which was rapidly flooding his apartment with water. Albert dropped his painting gear and hastened to his own place to fetch his plumbing equipment.

As he opened his front door, Albert heard strange sounds emanating from his father's bedroom: thuds, agonized cries, groans, more thuds. He dashed into the room, thinking that an intruder, perhaps a burglar, was attacking his father.

Instead, to his utter amazement, his father was standing in the middle of the room, stark naked, belabouring himself on the buttocks with a nail-studded paddle and masturbating himself with the other hand. With every stroke of the paddle he jumped into the air and cried out. Blood from his nail-punctured and beaten buttocks ran down his legs on to the floor. So engrossed was Fish in his self-inflicted torture that the arrival of his son upon the scene did not even register. He was quite oblivious of the younger man who stood upon the threshold, open-mouthed with horror. Albert was too dumbstruck to do or say anything. Albert grabbed his plumber's toolkit from his workshop and left as noiselessly as possible.

Later, he told his father that his thirty days in Bellevue did not seem to have done him any good. 'I admit that I'm a bit peculiar,' the old man replied in the understatement of the year. 'But I cannot help it. You'll have to learn to live with it.'

How Albert jun. managed to learn to cope was never made clear, but the older Fish soon after this incident reverted to his old pastime of sending obscene letters through the mail. Predictably, one of his more disgusting screeds found its way into police hands, passed on to them by an irate middle-aged widow who had advertised for a job as a housekeeper. Fish was quickly traced and arrested and spent the statutory ten days in Bellevue again for psychiatric evaluation. This time he was not kept longer in the hospital. In court, police described how they had found further unposted obscene letters stuffed under his mattress when they searched his room, and also related to an uncomprehending judge how they had found various objects in his room which would not be found in the room of a normal person. Asked what he used them for, the defendant replied, 'I stick them up my ass.' He was also asked to what use the whip was put. 'I whip myself with it,' Fish replied, 'and I don't see that it is your goddamned business what I do in my own room.' The judge agreed that what he did in private was no concern of the law, but that there *was* a law against offending decent citizens with filthy letters.

The psychiatric report from Bellevue had once more described Fish as 'quiet, co-operative and oriented' – and once again he was turned loose with a caution. On 5 September 1931 the crazed predator was back on the streets to prey on New York's children.

For some time thereafter, Fish had managed to steer clear of the attentions of the police. Albert jun. was hoping that the old man had learned a salutary lesson – or maybe age was taking its inevitable toll and dulling the macabre urges that assailed him. But as 1934 dawned, and spring came to Manhattan, Albert observed that his father's habits and general behaviour were becoming daily more bizarre. Eventually he wondered just how much more he could take before he would have to ask his father to move out into an apartment of his own. He could not even get a good night's sleep after a day's work – his father was now having recurrent nightmares when he would rave and shriek and even wake other tenants with the noise. He insisted on eating all meat raw and would fly into a towering rage if his son was cooking it. He also started using the floor of his room as a lavatory, and putting food out for a black cat which did not exist. He would leave the food until it was completely rotten, and then eat it himself. Remonstration got him nowhere, and Albert jun. was seriously concerned for both his and his father's health in such conditions. Yes, he would definitely have to go. The Bellevue doctors never saw him as he is now, mused Albert ruefully.

Unknown to him, his father had once again reverted to form with his campaign of obscene letter-writing. This time, however, he would not get off with a spell in Bellevue and an admonition from a judge who knew little of the world of sexual perversions. This time his activity would reveal the entire gamut of Fish's unimaginable depravities to a sickened world.

* * *

On 12 November 1934 Delia Budd, now living at the family's new apartment at 135 West 24th Street. The postmark indicated that it had been mailed from the Grand Central Post Office in Manhattan.

Delia Budd was uneducated and illiterate. She could barely make out her name on the envelope. Opening the letter, unable to read its contents, she called to her son Edward to read it to her. As the young man began to read it, he went as white as a sheet. 'What is it, Ted?' his mother cried in alarm. 'Is it bad news?' Edward did not answer but dashed from the apartment, leaving a mystified Delia. An hour later, Lieutenant King had the letter in his hands.

As the contents of most of this letter were so disgusting, I will quote a few passages only:

My dear Mrs Budd,
On Sunday June the 3rd 1928 I called on you at 406 W. 15th Street. I brought you pot cheese and strawberries as you may remember. We had lunch. Your daughter Grace sat on my lap and kissed me. I made up my mind to eat her, on the pretense of taking her to a party. You said yes, she could go. I took her to an empty house in Westchester I had already picked out. When we got there, I told her to remain outside. She picked wildflowers. I went upstairs and stripped all my clothes off … and when I was ready I called her. Then I hid in a closet until she was in the room. When she saw me all naked she began to cry and tried to run downstairs. I grabbed her and she said she would tell her mamma. First I stripped her naked. How she did kick, bite and scratch! I choked her to death, then cut her in small pieces so I could take the meat to my rooms, cook and eat it. How sweet and tender her little ass was roasted in the oven! It took me nine days to eat her entire body … She died a virgin.

Lieutenant King was exultant. After more than six years of blind alleys and dead ends, this must be, at long last, the breakthrough. However, it was not the letter itself but the envelope it had been sent in that proved to be the link connecting it with Fish. He was certain the letter was authentic, because it contained one or two details of the abduction known only to the police and not made public in the newspapers.

On the rear flap of the envelope was the small embossed logo of the New York Private Chauffeurs' Benevolent Association. A two-line address immediately below the logo had been crudely scratched through in ink. With the help of a magnifying glass, King deciphered it to read 627 Lexington Avenue, New York City. King thought the anonymous sender incredibly careless to use such an envelope with the address barely obscured and the logo not at all. King's visit to the Association failed to turn up any member named Howard in their records, but realizing that this could have been, and most probably was, an alias, the Lieutenant borrowed all the membership application forms – almost 400 – in order to compare them with the handwriting of the letter. He found no match.

Determined not to be fazed by this initial failure, King requested the secretary of the Association to call a meeting of all members. At this meeting the policeman gave a brief résumé of the Budd abduction and asked anyone who had purloined the association's stationery to come forward in confidence. He promised that no action would be taken in respect of the petty pilfering. After the meeting a part-time janitor/handyman who worked for the Association admitted to King that some six months earlier he had 'borrowed' a few sheets of headed paper and matching envelopes for his own use. Asked what he had done with them, the man said he had taken them home, but used only two. At that time he was living in a rooming-house at 200 East 52nd Street, in room number seven. King now asked him what he had done with the ones he did not use, and the man said he had just left them on a shelf in his room. They were still there when he moved out to his present abode a couple of months or so ago.

Mrs Frieda Schneider, the landlady, told King that after the NYPCBA janitor/handyman had vacated room number seven she had re-let the room to an old man who had stayed about two months and left only a few days ago. Shown one of the abduction circulars containing a detailed description of 'Frank Howard' she was immediately struck by the similarity of this description to that of her erstwhile lodger. 'He seemed a bit peculiar to me,' she offered. 'I was rather relieved when he went.' But she would not elaborate. King had the feeling, from knowing the contents of the letter, that Mrs Schneider was too embarrassed to specify her former lodger's peculiarities in detail, and he did not press her on this point.

Instead, King asked her to show him her register and point out the old man's signature, which read 'Albert H. Fish'. He took the letter from his pocket to compare the handwriting. It was identical.

Elated, King stressed the importance of apprehending Fish, and he asked for Mrs Schneider for any further information which might help towards this end. She suddenly remembered something which made the veteran officer's heart miss a beat. She said:

> He had a son working in North Carolina on a federal project. Every month this son would send him a check for twenty-five dollars. He was expecting one in about seven days' time and asked me to hold on to the letter for him as he did not yet know where he would be staying to let his son know the new address to send it to. He said he'd be coming to collect it in seven days or so.

King did not waste time but organized a round-the-clock stake-out. Fish took considerably longer than seven days to put in an appearance, and King thought that he might indeed have become aware of the stake-out, so he withdrew his men from the operation and instead instructed Mrs Schneider to call him at his office immediately Fish turned up. The call came on 13 December 1934. As instructed, she stalled her ex-lodger while King raced to the address in a fast car.

Mrs Schneider ushered King into the kitchen where Albert Fish, dressed in shabby, threadbare clothes, sat at a small side table getting to grips with a pot of tea and a plate of biscuits. He crossed the room in two strides. 'Albert Hamilton Fish?' he said.

Fish stood up and nodded. His wrists were so thin and bony that they almost slipped through the handcuffs. He went quietly with King to the car without a word, and Mrs Schneider, overcome with emotion, wept into the skirt of her apron and then poured herself a cup of tea.

* * *

Prior to his trial, Fish made a full confession not only to the murder of Grace Budd but also to a large number of hitherto unsolved murders and disappearances. He was at great pains to describe in the most revolting detail the ghastly mutilations he had committed on the bodies of his young victims. As well as regaling his interrogators with the nauseating details of how he cooked the various body parts and ate them, he also described his intense sexual reactions to these procedures. Hardened veteran detectives gagged at some of his disclosures, and – obsessive letter-writer that he was – if he felt that he had inadvertently omitted some particular item of this kind, he would set to and write a detailed description in a letter to the police officer, the counsel or the psychiatrist who had been interviewing him.

Even in jail while awaiting trial, Fish attempted to

continue with his bizarre self-torture. Guards used to light
his cigarettes for him, but one day he refused and insisted
on having matches so that he could light his own. This
made the guards suspicious and they searched his cell.
Hidden in the mattress they found cotton wool and a
bottle of alcohol which had been smuggled in, but they
were at a loss to know how this had occurred, as all his
visitors were searched.

On another occasion the lunch was a chicken joint and
when his plate was returned the bone was found to be
missing. Guards found that he had hidden it while plates
were being collected from the cells, after which he had
ground it to a sharp point on the concrete floor of his cell
and was caught cutting his buttocks with it while
masturbating with the other hand. His loud cries and
moans as he did so alerted the guards. He refused medical
attention to the cuts on his buttocks.

The trial of Albert Hamilton Fish opened on 12 March
1934 in the Westchester County Supreme Court in White
Plains, New York, before Judge Frederick P. Close. The
Chief Assistant District Attorney, Elbert D. Gallagher,
prosecuted, with another Assistant DA named Thomas
Scobie. Fish was defended by James Dempsey, with his
assistant Frank J. Mahoney. The previous day had been
taken up with the empanelling of jurors, which had been
an extremely difficult process. Many were dismissed for
personal reasons; one said he would not be willing to be
sequestered as his wife was unable to stoke the boiler!
Many were prejudiced by the known facts of the case and
would be even more likely to be so in the light of further
revelations. Eventually an all-male jury was empanelled,
eleven of the jurors being married men, and one a
bachelor. The jurors were warned that much of the
evidence would be of a most sordid and gruesome nature.
Nevertheless more than three hundred spectators, most of
them women, jammed the entrance hall of the court

clamouring for admission, and it took twelve deputies to keep the crowd in order. The public was admitted a few at a time until all the seats had been taken; no standing spectators were allowed. The Press tables were full, with representatives of major newspapers from world capitals as well as the main US cities. The New York tabloids would have a field-day and promised their readers the most hair-raising and macabre stories they would ever read. Their circulations were boosted by thousands of copies. Special additional copies had to be hurriedly printed.

At 10 a.m. Fish shuffled into the courtroom supported on either side by a deputy, and immediately it was the signal for a bevy of Press photographers to leap to their feet with cameras poised. Fish seemed to be dazzled by the exploding flash bulbs and attempted to shield his eyes with one bony hand. Judge Close immediately ordered all the photographers to leave the court, nor were they allowed to return during the remainder of the trial. They had to be content with shots taken outside the courtroom such as ones of Fish being led back to his cell, and of the judge and counsel leaving court. They were not allowed to photograph any of the jurors.

For the whole of the ten-day trial (this excludes the preliminary jury selection) Fish sat slumped in his chair at the defence table, displaying not the slightest apparent interest in the proceedings, not even when what the *New York Mirror* called 'the macabre revelations about this arch-fiend among fiends' were described in sickening detail. While jurors blanched visibly and the most squeamish of the spectators – men as well as women – fainted and had to be revived by court ushers, Fish sat, seemingly unmoved. He rested his head on his hand, elbow on the arm of his chair, and looked as though he had dozed off for much of the time. A columnist in the *Mirror* reported that he looked like 'a corpse insecurely propped in a chair'. And another undercover *Mirror* reporter who had been sitting in the public gallery *sans* notebook and pencil said that he had overheard the husband of one of the women who had fainted tell her afterwards, 'Edith, I *told* you not to come. I knew you wouldn't be up to it.'

Prosecutor Gallagher opened the trial with an outline of the abduction of Grace Budd by the defendant more than six years before, following this with a detailed narrative of Lieutenant King's untiring and relentless search, including the frustrating dead-end leads, the misidentified suspects, the clues that led nowhere. Until that morning of 11 November 1934 when Mrs Budd received that unspeakably vile letter from Fish. He then went on to describe the behind-the-scenes police activity generated by the accused's confessions, culminating in the finding of Grace Budd's discarded bones on the plot behind Wistaria Cottage in Westchester County, a deserted house to which Fish had taken his victim and where he had killed her.

The main point stressed in his opening argument was that Fish knew what he was doing and that he knew that what he was doing was wrong. That, Gallagher pointed out, was what constitutes sanity in the eyes of the law:

You will hear all manner of evidence, put into the record with the intention of convincing this court that this man is insane. He isn't. He knew what he was about. He knew that murder was against the law. He was sane enough to cover his tracks by using a false name, giving a false address and representing himself to be something other than he actually was. He was sane enough to choose an isolated location for the murder, and sane enough to return to it later to bury the bones of his victim. The proof, briefly, will be that this defendant is legally sane, the fact that he is indisputably a sexual psychopath notwithstanding.

Fish's defender, James Dempsey, based his case, predictably, on an insanity plea. This was certainly not difficult – with all the evidence of Fish's bizarre conduct Dempsey would not have his work cut out to put his client forward as a completely crazy madman. However, his task was fraught with one supreme problem: the jury would certainly be so revolted by the details that they as likely as not might well consider the crime so heinous that Fish should go to the chair anyway.

'We do not have to prove insanity,' Dempsey said. 'It is up to the State to prove otherwise. What we have to offer, nevertheless, is overwhelming proof that will demonstrate conclusively beyond any shadow of doubt that this man was insane as long ago as 1928 and is still insane to-day.'

Dempsey was scathing in his criticism of Bellevue Hospital which had discharged him as 'sane'. They were clearly in dereliction of their duty, Dempsey stressed, 'in freeing this man ... I submit that Bellevue has a lot to account for'. Dr Gregory was not in court but he must have read accounts of the trial in the newspapers, and his thoughts at that time can be more easily conjectured than described.

Members of the Budd family were the first prosecution witnesses. Delia Budd, her husband and her son Edward pointed to Fish and identified him positively as the 'Frank Howard' who had taken their daughter to the non-existent party at the non-existent address. While Delia Budd and her son remained impassive, Mr Budd broke down as he pointed a trembling finger at the old man. 'That is the man that took my child,' he said in a choked voice. 'That man right there.' He began to sob loudly, and was offered a glass of water. After he had composed himself, Gallagher asked him whether he had freely given his consent to the old man's proposition to take Grace to the party.

'He seemed so generous and kind ... I judged his appearance and personality and everything about him ...

He asked me and Mrs Budd would we give our permission, our consent ... He said that he would take very good care of her, and would return her no later than nine o'clock.'

'Did you give your consent?' Gallagher repeated.

'I gave my consent. Yes.' Mr Budd covered his face with his hands and sobbed. 'May God forgive me, yes.'

The witness was excused.

Lieutenant King was the last witness called to the stand that day. He described precisely how he had traced Fish to his former lodgings at 200 East 52nd Street and arrested him there when he called upon Mrs Schneider to collect the letter containing the cheque from his son John in North Carolina. The date of the arrest was 13 December 1934.

The court recessed for the day after King had given this testimony, just before 5 p.m., and the jury was sequestered in a local hotel.

Reconvening at 10 a.m. the following day, King was back on the stand to give the remainder of his evidence, which took most of that day. His account of Fish's confessions was far more lurid and less restrained than Gallagher's had been, and brought gasps of horror from jurymen and spectators alike. Newspaper reporters scribbled furiously on their pads, while Judge Close maintained a studied impartiality. One could only hazard a conjecture as to what he was thinking.

The high point came when court bailiffs carried into court a cardboard box containing the bones of Grace Budd. The effect on Dempsey was electric. Leaping to his feet, he shouted, 'I object, Your Honor! The testimony in this case is gruesome enough without putting the unfortunate victim's bones into evidence!'

'Objection overruled,' the judge replied calmly.

'Exception!' replied Dempsey angrily. 'May I note on the record the objection of the defense on the grounds that the introduction of this evidence ... would be highly prejudicial to the defendant. I submit that it is offered for the express purpose of inflaming the minds of the jury.'

'Objection overruled,' replied the judge.

'Exception!' shouted Dempsey. 'I call for a mistrial!'

The motion was denied, and the trial continued. Gallagher lifted the tiny skull from the box and held it aloft in full view of all present. Then he handed it to Lieutenant King. A portly middle-aged woman began to cry noisily and was ushered from the court by deputies.

Dempsey, still on his feet, strenuously objected, again calling for a mistrial 'by the very exhibition of this skull before the jury'. Judge Close overruled him. King continued with his evidence.

Dempsey's cross-examination of King commenced soon after the entering of the bones into evidence. He stressed the cannibalism admitted in the confessions, pointing out that no sane person could, or would, kill a little girl, dismember her and cut off portions of her body to be cooked and eaten. He also interrogated King at length about interviews he had had with Albert jun. and other members of the defendant's family regarding his bizarre behaviour and habits – a ploy clearly calculated to corroborate the validity of the insanity plea being put forward.

The following day of the trial saw a multiplicity of witnesses taking the stand, including Mrs Schneider, various police officers, Dr Amos Squire, the Medical Examiner who had autopsied the bones found behind Wistaria Cottage, the dentist who had compared his charts of dental work on Grace Budd's teeth with the teeth in the skull, and others who had played minor parts in the long search too numerous to mention here. Finally, three more of Fish's confessions were put into evidence: one to Captain John Stein, head of the Missing Persons Bureau who had succeeded Lieutenant King in this post, one to

Assistant DA of New York County P.F. Marro, and one to the former Westchester County DA, Frank Coyne. Predictably, Dempsey objected to all these and vociferously objected with more calls for a mistrial on the grounds that these confessions would prejudice and inflame the jury. Judge Close was by now becoming inured to the volatile Irishman's outbursts and calmly denied all his objections.

Dempsey had every reason to feel concern that his insanity defence was beginning to look a bit dodgy, as Gallagher read out these confessions. In one, Fish had expressed remorse after the murder; in another, he had described how he had avoided the police afterwards – in other words, he was fully aware that what he had done was wrong and in breach of the law.

On the Friday 15 May, the State rested its case after the final few witnesses had testified. James Dempsey was now about to electrify the already battered sensibilities of those in that courtroom by pulling his ace card out of the pack. He was not intending to take them through Grace Budd's abduction again – that had been done adequately already. Instead, he called to the stand Albert Fish jun. – a slightly built man who looked much younger than his thirty-five years. During his testimony he did not glance even once at his father – and neither did his father look at him. All too clearly, there was no love lost between the two, only bitterness and rancour.

Albert jun. described in graphic detail the forms the old man's madness had taken, which he had witnessed with his own eyes from as far back as 1922. These I have already referred to earlier in this chapter, so I need not repeat them here. The descriptions were calculated so as to leave no doubt in the minds of the jury that it was not just a sado-masochist they were dealing with but a madman.

Appropriately, the younger Fish was followed on the stand by the doctor who had X-rayed Fish in prison, who was able to produce the X-ray plates showing twenty-nine needles inserted into the man's lower body. Judging from the eroded condition of some of them, the doctor was able to confirm that Fish had been engaged in this practice for a good many years; others had been inserted, via the perineum, as recently as six months previous to the trial.

A surprise witness was Fish's married daughter, Mrs Gertrude DeMarco who, while agreeing that Fish treated his own family well and never raised a hand to any of them, knew that her father had several most peculiar habits, including sticking needles into his body. She had found out about this when he had sat at table one day squirming uncomfortably in his chair, and she had asked him whether he was having more trouble with a hernia he had recently suffered and for which he had undergone an operation.

'Oh, no,' he had replied. 'I have put three more needles inside me.'

'What did you do that for, pop?' I asked him.

'Well, you see, every so often I get this mood to do that and I cannot stop myself.' Mrs DeMarco was not asked what she thought about that ...

* * *

When the court reconvened on the morning of Monday 18 March, the jury having been sequestered over the weekend and doubtless wishing that the trial would soon be over, Judge Close, in view of the fact that the indescribably filthy letters Fish had written to various women were going to be read aloud as evidence, banned all women from the courtroom, amid howls of protest. As soon as the court had been cleared of all females, including two news reporters, Dempsey read to the court the letter which Fish had sent to one Mrs Grace Shaw, a middle-aged married woman who had advertised in the

New York Times offering to care for elderly boarders at her home in Queens. The contents of this letter were too obscene to be reproduced here. Another unsuspecting recipient of Fish's literary depravity was a Brooklyn landlady named Helen Karsen, who had suffered a similar indignity as far back as 1927. Yet a third was the much younger Mary Nicholas, who had naïvely agreed to meet her pen-pal but regretted it almost as soon as he had stepped across her threshold. Her father had chased him out after hearing his daughter scream. Fish had been sticking pins into his fingers, making them bleed, and was trying to force the girl to stick needles under his fingernails. It was 1930 and Mary was only twelve at the time.

Next to testify was Dr Fredric Wertham, the noted psychiatrist, who laid bare for all to see the bottomless pit of iniquity that made up the incomprehensible world of Albert Hamilton Fish – incomprehensible, that is, to normal people. Indeed, he admitted, some aspects of his psyche were incomprehensible even to himself. I have already mentioned some of the main points of Dr Wertham's testimony in the first few pages of this chapter. The jury, shocked already by earlier revelations of the trial, were positively catapulted out of their benumbed state into the bewilderment of being thrown into the knowledge of a dark world beyond their ken. But Dr Wertham did not flinch from what must have been, even for him, giving very unpleasant testimony.

After Wertham had concluded his testimony, Judge Close ordered the trial's first evening session. He aimed to have the case in the jury's hands by the weekend. After a recess for dinner, the court reconvened at 7.30 p.m. for Dempsey's two further expert witnesses to add their testimony to that of Dr Wertham. One amplified this by describing Fish's many hallucinations and pseudo-religious visions, or 'visitations' as Fish called them; the other tended to concentrate more on the sexual element. Fish, he testified, had insisted that Grace Budd had died a virgin, but he admitted that he had experienced two emissions as he choked her to death. He had told the doctor that the girl's frantic struggles had precipitated his intense sexual excitement, but that 'that was nothing compared to the degree of sexual excitement I experienced during the nine days I was consuming her body'.

Dempsey's and Gallagher's respective final speeches more or less recapitulated what they had already said during the long days of the trial. Dempsey ended his with an impassioned appeal for mercy for 'this abject lunatic, this maniac who cannot be in his right mind to have been able to commit such repulsive atrocities for more than fifty years'. He went on to continue his attack on Bellevue for their criminal negligence, and he also laid part of the blame on Mr and Mrs Budd for allowing their 10-year-old child to go off with a complete stranger. Finally, he appealed to the jurors' sensibilities, 'I ask you, gentlemen – now that you have heard all the evidence ... do you believe, before God, that Albert Fish was sane on the third day of June 1928? Do you honestly believe that on that day he knew right from wrong?'

In complete contrast to Dempsey's summation, Gallagher's was a model of restraint, a recapitulation of hard facts, an averral that no reasonable man could but find Fish guilty. Gallagher emphasized again how cunning and pre-planned Fish had been in the carrying out of his perverted purpose, which was to commit this crime. The issue was a simple one, boiled down to basic essentials: did Albert Fish kill Grace Budd and, if so, did he know that what he was doing was wrong? It was fully agreed by both sides that the defendant *had* killed Grace Budd. All the jury now had to decide was whether this perverted fiend was in full possession of his senses at the time. 'The defense has referred to Albert Fish as a poor, pathetic, defenseless old man. I would ask you, gentlemen, to remember the poor, pathetic, defenseless child Grace Budd as she screamed and struggled in the springtime of her life and said that she would tell her mamma.'

Judge Close began his charge to the jury immediately after the court reconvened after the lunch recess. His summation was ordered, concise and clear. He recited at length several sections of the penal code, with special reference to the law on the question of insanity, elucidating all the points which could have any possible bearing on the case. 'A morbid propensity to commit prohibited acts,' he explained, 'existing in the mind of a person who is not shown to have been incapable of knowing the wrongfulness of such acts, is no defense.' He went on to repeat the legal definition of insanity as set out under the M'Naghten Rule. Many of those in court construed the judge's summing-up as being biased in favour of a guilty verdict, but others saw his admonitions as being no more than doing his duty as a jurist to set out plainly the law's stance on the question of insanity to guide the jury in making an informed decision.

Just after three o'clock Judge Close ended his charge:

Well, now, gentlemen, if you find that this man through his own perversion has so weakened his will that an irresistible impulse comes upon him to satisfy his sexual passions, that would not excuse him from the consequences of his act. He must have been suffering from such a defect of reason as not to know the nature and quality of his act or to know that it was wrong when he performed it, or he must answer for the consequences of his act.

At six o'clock the jury recessed for dinner, and commenced their deliberations at 7.30 p.m. In just under one hour they had arrived at a unanimous verdict. 'We find the defendant guilty of murder as charged in the indictment,' the foreman declared. Murder in the first degree carried a mandatory sentence of death in the electric chair at Sing Sing.

Fish stood impassive at the sentence, and had nothing to say after the pronouncement of the verdict. Guards led him out past the bevy of newsmen to return him to his cell, and again he seemed to be dazed by the flashing bulbs.

Fish's family heard the news as they stood in the hallway outside the courtroom. His sons were silent, but his daughters broke into loud sobs and were shepherded from the court building by their husbands.

Reporters asked the Budds for their reactions. Mrs Budd was jubilant. 'Just what I expected – good!' she said. Mr Budd echoed her sentiments. 'He deserves the chair,' he said. 'All that insanity lark was bunk!'

Edward concurred. 'The verdict was a just one,' he said. 'It won't bring Grace back, but he got what he deserved.'

Inevitably, Dempsey was besieged by newsmen for his reactions to the verdict. 'The man is insane!' he said. 'As mad as a hatter. I just cannot conceive how twelve intelligent men, in the face of this overwhelming evidence of perversion, which makes him an incredible pervert even among perverts, could decide he was sane.' He shook his head in utter disbelief.

Reporters catching up with the jurors outside the courthouse building as they made their way home, thankful that at last the trial was over and they could rejoin their families, were informed unequivocally that they, the jurors, had also thought Fish was insane, but that they felt he should die in the chair anyway for such a heinous crime.

The tabloids had more shocks for the reading public during the days following the trial. Fish had confessed to a gruesome string of ghastly murders which had remained in the unsolved files until now. After all, he was reported as saying, if he was going to the chair anyway, what did he have to lose? He might just as well clear up some at least of the more recent cases.

Billy Gaffney, just four years old, had been abducted in February 1927. He had been seen with a small crying boy on a tram – the conductor remembered him. The boy's body, hideously mutilated with the face beyond recognition, had been found on a public rubbish tip in Riker Avenue in Astoria. Fish had sliced flesh from his body, including his face, and taken it home to cook in a stew. Before he had killed the boy, he had subjected him to various fiendish tortures.

The boy had been identified from a pile of his clothing that had been found near the body, but his killer had never been found.

In 1924 Fish had killed 8-year-old Francis McDonnell on Staten Island, luring him into a wooded lot and strangling him with his own braces. He was about to dismember the body when he heard the sound of someone approaching, and fled. The boy was the son of a policeman. Only now, ten years on, was this killing solved as Fish related the grisly details to three senior lawmen in Sing Sing. By the time he had reached the end of his confessions, fifteen hitherto unsolved child homicides had been corroborated by Fish, giving details that only the killer could have known.

On the Monday 25 March, Fish was brought from prison to be formally sentenced to die in the electric chair by Judge Close. The date was set for some time during the week of 29 April. On the judge's pronouncing the sentence, Fish replied, 'Thank you, Your Honour.'

Three days after this, one night a prison guard failed to notice that the bone from the pork chop Fish had received for supper was not on the plate as it was being removed. It was not until the next day that another guard found the prisoner mutilating himself with the bone, which he had ground to a point. Even prison, and the spectre of death in the chair, had failed to curb his perverted lusts.

On 3 April Dempsey filed for a reversal of Fish's conviction on several legal grounds, including the prosecutor's display of the bones of Grace Budd to the jury, and also what he considered to be the hostility of the trial judge to the defence, but most of all he cited what he called the 'self-evident proof' of Fish's insanity. He quoted a list of no fewer than seventeen sexual perversions which Dr Wertham had prepared for him, all of which were practised by Fish and some of which were, as he put it, 'hitherto unheard of'. Fish, Dempsey declared, was a 'psychiatric phenomenon'. 'It is noteworthy,' he said, 'that no single case history report, either in legal or medical annals, contains a record of one individual who possessed all of these sexual abnormalities.'

Fish's execution had of course been stayed pending appeal, but the Court of Appeal dismissed it and the death sentence was upheld. The execution date was rescheduled for the week of 13 January 1936. Dempsey made one final bid for clemency in a meeting with the Governor of New York, enlisting in his aid Dr Wertham, who moved that if Fish were committed to a secure institution for the criminally insane, the medical profession would have a chance to study the man's psychological makeup and learn something that might help prevent crimes against children. Governor Herbert Lehman remained unmoved, unimpressed by the doctor's arguments, and Dempsey left his office, a dejected man.

On 16 January 1936, at 11 a.m., Fish was strapped into the electric chair at Sing Sing. Those present were unprepared for what happened: the needles embedded in the old man's body short-circuited the current, causing blue sparks to emanate from the contact points, and a second shock had to be administered. This time, the electrocution apparatus worked, and at 11.09 a.m. Fish was pronounced dead by the prison doctor.

Bad or mad? Who was right – Gallagher or Dempsey? What do you think? For myself, I am inclined to believe that he was a combination of both.

10

Folie à Deux

Douglas Clark and Carol Bundy (1983)

If there can be anything more terrifying than a crazed serial killer loose on the streets, then it must be *two* crazed serial killers acting in concert. Such a pair was Douglas Daniel Clark and his girlfriend Carol Bundy. She was no relation whatsoever to the notorious Ted Bundy, but no doubt she rejoiced in bearing the same name as the killer of twenty-eight verified victims and possibly more, whose killing spree had preceded her own by about ten years.

Douglas Clark was the son of a former high-ranking naval officer who had afterwards gone into engineering consultancy on an international scale. As a direct result of this, young Douglas, who was born in 1948, was raised not just in one country of domicile but in no fewer than thirty-seven different countries. It is a great and abiding shame that this mind-broadening experience did not, unfortunately, do him much good.

After dropping out of high school, Clark took a variety of menial jobs for short periods – he was never a stayer – interspersed with living on his wits, pimping, living at the expense of lonely middle-aged females and the odd burglary or two. His preferred occupation was that of gigolo. He entertained fantasies of torture, killing and mutilation, paedophilia and necrophilia – but these obscene lusts were all in his head. Until he met Carol Bundy.

He met her in a tavern called the Little Nashville, in North Hollywood, California. Carol had been madly in love with the manager of her apartment building, an Australian immigrant named John Murray, forty-five, who sang country and western songs in the aforesaid bar. Clark was immediately attracted to Carol, a 37-year-old woman of buxom proportions. Although Carol had already broken up with Murray, she still carried a torch for him and sat most nights in the bar nursing a beer just so she could watch him and enjoy his singing; he had a good voice.

Clark at that particular time was working in the boiler room of a soap factory in suburban Burbank. How he worked with the boilers is anybody's guess, but he was certainly a fast worker where Carol was concerned. Before that night was out he had literally swept her off her feet and moved into her apartment. He became the love of her life right from the word go. Whoever said that finding a new love is the best way to get over an old one, was certainly right as far Carol Bundy was concerned.

Carol had an eyesight problem, but had done nothing about it. Clark took her to a social security office and had her declared officially registered partially sighted, which entitled her to an allowance of 620 dollars a month for her and her two little boys from her failed marriage. He then took her to an optometrist where she was fitted with contact lenses which improved her sight to a considerable degree. Carol enjoyed the domestic chores of looking after Doug as well as the children. Unfortunately the unscrupulous Doug was more interested in using her money and her car to enable him to indulge in his fantasies than in settling down as a family man. But his tremendous sexual prowess – to use Carol's own description – every night more than compensated her for his shortcomings.

Once Doug felt that he was firmly ensconced in the Bundy household, he felt that he could allow his fantasies a freer rein. Carol was not the inhibited type and he started tentatively by giving voice to some of his less far-out mind-wanderings during sex. She seemed receptive enough – at least she was not shocked. So he decided to go a bit further to test her reactions. He brought an 11-year-old girl home with him. She was no innocent lamb but streetwise and toying with the idea of going on the game.

Doug told Carol that whatever he did with the young girl would be with her consent; what he wanted Carol to do was to take some Polaroid shots of her in the nude, which she did. He then suggested that he have the girl perform oral sex upon him while Carol took further photographs, that would spice up their love life a bit. Carol agreed, but only at the cost of stifling her natural feelings of revulsion. What had gotten into Doug? She knew he had some weird sexual fantasies, but this was a bit over the top. Still, she had better not make too much of a fuss or he might get annoyed and knock her about – he had already shown a few violent streaks. Worse, he might leave her. She loved him to distraction and dared not risk that.

After the girl had left the apartment, promising not to blab to anybody and clutching a dollar bill in her hand, Doug turned to Carol. 'Now wasn't that terrific?' he said. 'You know what I'd really like, don't you? I'd like to kill a girl and have sex with her dead body. What do you think of that?'

'I'm not going to tell you what I think,' Carol hedged

evasively. 'What you'd like to do, is up to you. I bet you
wouldn't dare anyway.'

'Oh yeah? I would if I wanted to, mark my words!'

Carol dismissed his boasting as just so much macho
bravado, but when two young teenage girls went missing
on 11 June 1980 and she observed Doug smirking as he
watched the item about their disappearance on the TV
news programme, she began to wonder. But she did not
need to wonder for long: Doug, without any questions or
prompting, gloatingly confessed to her that he had killed
them. He described to her how he had forced both girls,
15-year-old Gina Narano and her 16-year-old half-sister
Cynthia Chandler, to perform oral sex upon him and how
he had shot each girl through the head just at his point of
climax. He then told Carol that he would kill her two boys
if she ever went to the police or, indeed, told anybody.

The girls' bodies were found the following morning
beside the Ventura Freeway in suburban Griffith Park, Los
Angeles. From this day forward Carol Bundy knew that
she was on a roller-coaster to disaster; even if she herself
did not betray her homicidal maniac of a lover to the
authorities, Nemesis would be bound to catch up with
him eventually – and what could she say? That she had no
knowledge of Doug's deadly activities?

Thirteen days later, a 24-year-old prostitute was found
shot dead behind a Burbank restaurant in the early hours
by an employee taking out garbage, and later that same
morning another hooker – minus her head – was
discovered by a man going to work in Studio City. That
afternoon Carol's two sons were visiting relatives in a
nearby suburb, and she was with Doug in the kitchen. 'I
have a surprise for you,' he said. Opening the fridge, he
removed a human head. It was the head of the decapitated
hooker. Placing it on the kitchen worktop, Doug ordered
Carol to wash the hair and make up the face with
cosmetics. Carol's thoughts as she did his bidding are not

recorded, but even she, besotted as she was with Clark, must have felt nauseated by her grisly task, even if she did not protest. She is on record as having said, 'We had a lot of fun with her. I was making her up like a Barbie with shampoo and makeup'. Doug then took the head into the shower for oral sex.

Three days later a man was driving home when he found the entrance to his garage obstructed by a wooden box. He got out of his car to move it and was annoyed that someone should have used his driveway to dump their rubbish. He looked into the box to see what it was that had been so inconsiderately discarded, and gasped with horror to see a girl's head staring up at him with sightless, eye-shadowed and mascaraed eyes.

On 30 June a group of snake-hunters in thick woodland near Sylmar, in the San Fernando valley, came upon the badly decomposed body of a 17-year-old girl, later identified as Marnette Comer, a runaway from Sacramento, who had been missing since 1 June. Forensic examination showed that she had been dead at least three weeks.

There was to be no let-up in Clark's deadly rampage. On 25 July the body of a young girl, shot through the head, was found on Sunset Boulevard. She was never identified, and remains in police records as a 'Jane Doe'. Near Malibu another unidentified female corpse was discovered, killed with a small-calibre bullet to the head like her predecessors. Forensic pathologists found that all four of these last victims had been raped after death as well as orally abused.

Doug made no secret of his nocturnal outrages to the compliant Carol Bundy. But she was obviously feeling the strain of being the enforced confidante of her evil paramour, because she now began to resume her patronage of the 'Little Nashville' bar and talk to John Murray over their beer. It seemed she became somewhat loose-lipped when the worse for wear, as she was not a heavy imbiber and was not used to doing a lot of drinking. It seems that in unguarded moments she let slip a few hints about Doug's involvement in the reported crimes. Murray urged her to go to the police, saying that if she would not, then he would. Panicked by this situation, Carol told him that they should meet specifically to discuss this situation and what they should do, but in private, not in the bar. They agreed a meeting in Murray's van at midnight on 5 August.

There she shot him through the head with her own 9mm Beretta pistol – a weapon small enough to be carried in a handbag, which is why it is sometimes known as the 'ladies' gun'. Afterwards she cut off his head with a small saw for good measure (her handbag must have been one of the bigger kind). Prior to the killing she and Murray had sex. Perhaps this may have been to allay his suspicions, rather than from any great degree of desire on her part. The killing was obviously to prevent Murray from carrying out his threat to report Clark to the police ('I did this for Doug,' she later testified at the trial. 'Everything I did was for Doug. I loved him and him only. I still do.')

The decapitation was something else again. Obviously, once Murray had been shot dead he could not carry out his threat, so sawing his head off would serve no useful purpose. Carol Bundy, unlike Doug, did not get any sexual thrill from such an act. It can therefore safely be assumed that she did this so that she could brag to Clark that she was just as capable of carrying out such an atrocity as he was – a sort of level pegging in crime. He would then respect her more, in a twisted kind of way. They were in this together now, through thick and thin …

When John Murray was not available at his apartment to meet the needs of the tenants in his building, no one thought anything amiss, as he was just as liable to take one or two days off as anyone else. The Australian was an affable type who would never make an issue of a tenant's being a few days late with his rent, though if someone had an urgent repair needed such as a leaking pipe or a clogged toilet, he would have to call an outside plumber. Similarly, at the 'Little Nashville' bar, the country and western singer would be missed, but would just be presumed to have taken a short holiday. He had left his guitar in its usual locker.

August is very hot in California and three days after Murray dropped from sight his van, which was still parked behind the bar, began calling attention to itself from the hordes of flies which started swarming around it. On the fourth day police were called after a customer leaving the bar complained of a foul stench which he said seemed to be coming from the parked vehicle.

Despite strenuous efforts on the part of the police, no one was apprehended in the course of hunting for a suspect in the Murray slaying, and the middle-aged, overweight blonde who had so often been seen sitting at a table with him between songs was certainly not even in the frame. It was known that they had once been lovers and were still close friends even though the girl now had a new man in her life. It was most unlikely, police thought, that she would kill him. To their knowledge, the two had had no quarrel, or even a disagreement.

Clark and Bundy were still free to carry on with their fiendish rampage throughout suburban Hollywood. A 17-year-old hitchhiker was abducted at gunpoint, shot and sexually abused and discarded in the rugged Tuna Canyon area, where Bundy later said that she had thrown Murray's head, although this was never found. The girl's body was not discovered until several months later. After Clark had killed the girl, he drove back home to show Carol the body before driving off to deposit it in the canyon. The risks he took were incredible. Just about anybody could have happened to pass by in the side street where, in broad daylight, he showed Carol the corpse as it lay in his car, before driving off.

A few days after this, Clark and Bundy were cruising around a neighbourhood shopping complex looking for potential victims. In the car park they enticed a young teenage girl into their car. Only a few moments later she managed to wrench open the car door and fell out on to the concrete, bleeding from a dozen slash and stab wounds and shrieking at the top of her voice. As horrified shoppers rushed to her aid, the car containing the lethal pair roared off at speed with a screech of tyres, knocking over two litter bins and scraping another car. It was being driven too fast to enable spectators to read even part of the licence plate. All they were able to see was that it was a dark-coloured, older model compact.

The girl who had had such a fortunate escape from the crazed duo was able to give the police a good description of the man and woman, though not of the car – she was not very knowledgeable about cars, she said. Although the police issued a BOLO (be on the lookout) for the couple and their vehicle, no suspects were forthcoming.

All this time, however, things were getting a bit too much for Carol Bundy. In her youth she had trained as a nurse, and had been nursing in state hospitals until the birth of her two children. Now that her boys were old enough to attend school, Carol had taken a part-time position as an agency nurse in a convalescent home for the elderly in Van Nuys, the suburb where she and Clark had moved to a bigger apartment.

One day, after a particularly strenuous bout of duty, things came to a head. Carol, who enjoyed the friendship of her immediate supervisor, whom she had known for twenty years, felt everything boiling up inside her. She suddenly burst into a flood of tears as she was sitting in the canteen with her friend talking over coffee. 'I can't take it any more!' she gasped between racking sobs. 'I'm supposed to save lives, not take them!'

'Hey, honey, take it easy!' the supervisor comforted, putting an arm round her friend's shoulder. 'What do you mean?'

Carol sobbed out a hysterical tale of murder and mayhem with her live-in lover Douglas Clark.

The supervisor did not know what to think. It seemed unlikely that the woman would make up a story as horrendous as this. Yet she had known Carol since she first entered the nursing world, and had kept up the friendship while Carol took the years off to raise her children until school age. She would never in her wildest imaginings have considered Carol to be the type of woman to throw in her lot with a serial killer, never mind shoot a man and cut off his head. Carol did not take drugs, so they could not be at the bottom of all this. Yet the story had the ring of truth.

'Would you like me to talk to the police for you?' the supervisor asked. 'You could take the rest of the day off. Doug wouldn't be at home, would he?'

'No, he'd be at work in Burbank,' Carol replied.

'Good. Then the police can pick him up there for questioning and get all this sorted out.'

Which is precisely what they did, arresting him on the job. Hidden under one of the boilers he tended, they found his .22 mm pistol. Later the same day they called upon Carol in Van Nuys. She was calmer now. They told her that she had nothing to fear, that Clark was safely locked up in jail. She gave her consent for the officers to search the apartment, which revealed startling evidence in the form of albums full of Polaroid photographs of nude teenage girls, mostly in pornographic poses and some of them engaged in pornographic acts with Clark. These included the 11-year-old girl who had been lured to the apartment at the beginning of Clark's relationship with Carol Bundy.

Even more damning, however, was the finding of bloodstains in various parts of the flat, which forensic experts were able to match to the blood groups of Gina Marano and Cynthia Chandler.

Clark was made of sterner stuff than Bundy and refused to say anything; he would not even admit that the gun found under the boiler was his, saying someone else must have left it there, possibly the previous boilerman. But Bundy continued to talk. She admitted killing Murray, contributing to the murder of an unidentified hooker, and participating in the stabbing and slashing of the victim in the car park who had survived. She also did not deny knowledge of Clark's other murders.

Carol had thought that by testifying against Clark she would be allowed to plea-bargain a greatly reduced sentence for her own crimes, but in this she was doomed to disappointment ...

In January 1983 Clark was sent for trial before Justice Ricardo A. Torres. On 28 January the jury found him guilty of six counts of first-degree murder and a number of other indictments including attempted murder, sexual offences and the offence of mutilating human remains. Evidence had linked bullets found in the heads of five of Clark's known victims to the gun found in the boiler room, and three pairs of women's briefs found in his apartment to three of the victims.

Clark denied the murders and callously laid the blame on Carol Bundy, saying that Murray had been her accomplice and that she had shot him when he had proposed to turn himself in. But the jury was not fooled by his arrogant lies. On 15 February he was sentenced to die in the gas chamber at San Quentin.

Carol Bundy went to her own trial, also before Judge Ricardo A. Torres, shortly after her lover's trial had ended. Unlike Clark, who had represented himself, Carol had a court-appointed attorney to argue her case, which was that she had acted under duress from Clark. This plea did little to help her, however. Indicted in the first place for her admitted murder of Murray, for which she was arrested, further charges were brought of complicity in the murder of the unidentified hooker, attempted murder of the girl in the car park, and of complicity by handing her gun to Clark when his own gun had jammed, in the case of another of the killings.

Carol Bundy burst into tears as she was sentenced. She had been certain in her own mind that judge and jury would consider her to have been more sinned against than sinning, but she was sadly mistaken. Judge Torres sentenced her to twenty-seven years to life on the charge of murdering Murray and twenty-five years to life on the other charges, the sentences to run consecutively.

11

A Quarter Million Dollars Bail

Richard Cottingham (1979)

New York's firemen are used to grisly sights during the course of their work. Dangerous and unpleasant work at the best of times, what with the heat, the flames, the scaling of ladders and the emission of clouds of acrid smoke and poisonous fumes from burning plastic and foam furniture stuffing, they also not infrequently have to contend with charred corpses of fire victims. So they are not unused to such things, and are prepared.

Nothing, however, could have prepared fireman Don Mecklenberg for the sight that met his questing gaze as he crawled on all fours across the floor of a smoke-filled room in a seedy, run-down hotel in New York's West 42nd Street, not far from Times Square, which was ablaze. Vaguely visible to him was a figure lying on a bed, towards which he was inching his way. He managed to reach the figure and drag it out of the room into the corridor outside, and was about to render mouth-to-mouth resuscitation when he realized with a jolt of revulsion that the figure was the headless corpse of a girl,

155

whose hands had also been severed. Stifling the urge to vomit, he returned to the room to ascertain whether there was anyone else there, alive or dead. In the far corner, on another bed, was another female figure, nude like the first, and similarly decapitated and handless. This time Don barely made it to the corridor before throwing up.

The fire was considered by the police and fire service investigators to be arson, a view which was confirmed when forensic pathologists discovered that petrol lighter fluid had been poured on the lower body of each of the two victims. Headless and handless bodies are, of course, much more difficult to identify than complete corpses, and one of the two females defied identification. She was white, aged around eighteen or nineteen, and ended up in the city morgue with a 'Jane Doe' tag tied to her toe, with the location and the date – 2 December 1979.

The other female would prove easier to identify, since she was of Middle Eastern appearance and would have records in police files of aliens' immigration registrations. X-rays of her bones were taken and compared with hospital records for young women immigrants, and came up with a match from a limb fracture. The girl was 22-year-old Deedeh Goodarzi, a native of Kuwait. Beautiful, with black eyes and long, dark hair, she had been a graduate from a high school in Long Island, but for some unfathomable reason had dropped out, thrown away her opportunity of attending college, and taken up the life of a prostitute in the sleazy 42nd Street district of New York City. She had notched up three citations for prostitution in police files, as well as one for a petty theft. Known to her clients as 'Dee-Dee', she had also worked in a massage parlour in Atlantic City, providing so-called 'special services' for the customers.

The lower torsos of both victims had been badly burned, and it was thought that the same person who had set the bodies alight had also set fire to their room. It was considered likely that the unidentified victim was also a prostitute, who had shared a room in the hotel with the Kuwaiti girl. Inquiries were set afoot among the area's streetwalkers and pimps to try to ascertain whether a young white girl was missing from her usual haunts, but no leads were forthcoming from this angle. A pile of clothes, found in the bathroom adjoining the victims' room, were assumed to have been worn by the victims before they had been stripped, but none of the items was recognized by those questioned.

The missing heads and hands were never found, despite an intensive search, and the conclusion was drawn by police investigators that the killer had disposed of them in the garbage collection system which operated daily in the teeming city.

The hookers of 42nd Street and the Times Square district were scared – no doubt about it. They carried Mace, stilettos, even handguns. They scrutinized carefully the men who provided them with their livelihood, avoiding anybody who seemed in the least dodgy – there were so many weirdos about, one never could tell. Being smartly dressed and well-spoken was no guarantee that a man did not harbour fantasies of bondage, flagellation or some other perversion. Hookers were murdered almost every day all over the United States. Serial killers were becoming an epidemic. The world's oldest profession was also the one most fraught with danger. Yet girls, often only in their early teens, continued to ignore the warnings. Some peddled their bodies to fund their drug habit. And now, once again, two more of the sisterhood had paid the dreadful price.

As they talked among themselves in fearful whispers, the hookers were convinced that the same man had killed Helen Sykes, a teenage runaway from California, who had worked in an area very close to the fleapit hotel where Deedeh Goodarzi and her companion had been found.

Helen's body had been found in January of that year in Queens, spreadeagled on the sidewalk in the early hours, by a man on his way to work. Her head had been almost severed from her body, and her legs had been cut off and carried a block from where she was found, and laid out side by side in a seemingly ritualistic fashion. The prostitutes were not the only ones who had put two and two together and come up with the right number – the police were quick to link the latest slayings with Helen's murder, for pathologists had averred that the same surgical skill had been used to decapitate and remove the hands of the two fire victims as had been used to almost decapitate the January victim and to sever her legs. They considered it very likely, also, that the same instrument had been used – a double-edged thin steel-bladed knife.

Police were no nearer a solution to the three baffling murders when they were called to a motel in Hasbrouck Heights, in New Jersey, where a horrified chambermaid, entering one of the rooms to make up the bed and clean the room for the next occupant, discovered the naked body of a girl stuffed under one of the twin beds. The girl, teenaged Valerie Street, had been strangled, savagely beaten and mutilated; a nipple had almost been bitten off, and her breasts had been slashed and gnawed by human teeth. The police had no doubt that it was the work of the same man who had killed the other three women, despite the different location. The killer's *modus operandi*, however, was the same.

The police were also not slow to note the decrease of the intervals of time between the slayings – a phenomenon that is a well-known characteristic of serial killers. From January to December had been about a year; from December to 5 May, when the New Jersey victim was found, was only about five months. The next time interval would be only ten days …

On 15 May another prostitute, Jean Reyner, was found

stabbed to death in a 29th Street hotel near Times Square. Her breasts had been sliced off with the same surgical skill that had been evident to the forensic investigators who had examined the corpses of the first three victims. She had also been set on fire in the same way as the December victims, with petrol lighter fluid, although the fire had burned itself out and the room where she was found had not been set alight.

While the newspapers and TV reports dubbed the unknown killer 'Jack the Ripper' reincarnated to terrorize the hookers of New York just as he had terrorized the streetwalkers of London's East End in 1888, the police were frantically trying to solve the crimes, unaware that another seven days would provide them with the breakthrough they so sorely needed, and in the same place where the New Jersey victim had been found. On 22 May they were called again to the motel in Hasbrouck Heights in response to reports of a woman screaming. Leaping from his car with gun drawn, Patrolman Floyd Griffith was just in time to apprehend a smartly groomed man in a business suit, carrying a large black leather briefcase, who charged from the motel to flee on foot to his car which he had left in a side street a short distance away. Colleagues spilled from the police cruiser to come to the officer's aid, subduing the suspect, handcuffing him and bundling him unceremoniously into the car, while other officers ran into the building.

There in one of the rooms they found a hysterical young girl, stark naked and handcuffed to a bedpost, covered with blood, being comforted by a maid. She had been raped, sodomized and orally abused, beaten and slashed, and her breasts had been bitten. Rushed to hospital, she was sedated and treated for her injuries, but it was some days before she became calm enough to relate to the police investigators what had happened to her.

She had arrived only a few days previously – a runaway

of fifteen from a small West Coast town – and had almost immediately met a pimp who promised her 'the good life' – a misnomer if ever there was one – if she would work the streets for him. She had met this well-dressed 'john' who had taken her to one of the area's better restaurants for dinner, including wine, and then taken her to the motel. Once there, he changed from a pleasant and well-spoken businessman to a raging maniac. The naïve and inexperienced girl had learned the hard way that a good outward appearance was not necessarily synonymous with normal behaviour and that the apparently likeable young man was in reality a fiend in human form.

The 33-year-old man who had fled from the motel literally straight into the arms of the law was a most unlikely suspect. He was Richard Francis Cottingham, head of the computer department of the Blue Cross – Blue Shield Insurance Company, a major Manhattan firm. A native of Lodi, New Jersey, he still lived in that town, in a detached white house set in spacious landscaped gardens. His neighbours thought of him as a model husband and father of three children. They told police that he was always very polite and courteous, but kept himself to himself and did not socialize very much. His employers likewise had only a good word to say for him and pointed out his unblemished work record at the firm where he had worked for the past thirteen years. The police, therefore, were more than a little surprised, to say the least, when they began to uncover their suspect's sinister secret life.

To start with, the black briefcase he was carrying when he was arrested did not contain business papers, computer print-outs or suchlike items. It contained three sets of handcuffs, a black leather face mask so fashioned as to include a gag, two black leather 'slave collars' fitted with pointed chrome studs on their inner surface, a whip, two slender double-edged blades set into ivory handles, and several small phials of chloral hydrate (a knockout drug). There was also a small non-working replica handgun, so realistic that none of the girls who had been forced to commit various perverse acts at 'gunpoint' would have known it was not the real thing. In his pockets were the key to the motel room, keys to other rooms in unidentified locations, three petrol lighters (although he was a non-smoker), and a switchblade.

Cottingham was taken into custody without further ado and a warrant issued to search his home. In his private rooms the investigators found a veritable den of iniquity: hundreds of pornographic photographs, a Polaroid camera, female undergarments, purses, cosmetics and jewellery taken from his victims, magazines featuring torture and bondage, flagellation and other sado-masochistic practices.

Police investigations revealed that Cottingham's wife had filed for divorce about a month prior to his arrest, citing extreme cruelty, gross sexual misconduct, attempting to force her to take part in deviant acts, failure to maintain her and their children, and failure to perform normal marital obligations. He had also been cautioned, according to police records, on two occasions in the early 1970s, in respect of public order offences involving prostitutes.

The following day he appeared in court charged with the attempted murder of the young teenage hooker in the New Jersey motel. The judge ordered him to be kept in custody by setting bail at a cool quarter of a million dollars. 'You are not safe to be at large,' he said. No one could argue with that!

It was not long before the police were busy compiling a long list of additional charges. He was indisputably tied to the murders of Deedeh Goodarzi and her nameless partner in death, to the murders of Valerie Street and Helen Sykes, and to the murder of Maryann Carr, a 26-year-old nurse, who had been found strangled in

December 1977 in the very same motel in Hasbrouck Heights which had been the scene of two of his later crimes. The nurse had her hands and feet tied and her breasts mutilated when she was found. It had taken the police more than two years to solve her murder.

The tabloids were having a field day describing the 'Jekyll and Hyde' who was a model husband and father, an exemplary employee by day and a raving lunatic by night who tortured, raped and killed prostitutes to satisfy his abnormal and perverted lusts. Even as banner headlines blared out Cottingham's murder charges, the police were compiling still further indictments on an assortment of kidnapping and abduction offences, rape charges and lesser assaults, including offences against women who had survived his murderous attacks and lived to testify in court.

Some of these attacks were only less hideous than the murders in that the victims had not been killed. In one case, a pregnant 22-year-old waitress had been lured into a car, where she was offered, and accepted, drinks. Unknown to her, these had been spiked with a powerful knockout drug. When she awoke, she was in a room somewhere and her abductor was beating her with a rubber hose. She then drifted back into unconsciousness. When she finally awoke, her tormentor was gone, and so was all her clothing, purse, money and jewellery – even her earrings and rings had been removed. She was lying naked on the floor of a motel room in South Hackensack, New Jersey, and was bleeding from the vagina, rectum and mouth, and her breasts had been bitten and were also bleeding. She was so shocked by the assault that she was quite unable to remember her abductor's appearance or anything about his car, so the police had very little to go on in searching for a suspect at the time.

Another pregnant woman, a housewife, had gone into a neighbourhood bar for a drink when a personable young man joined her and started to chat. They then moved to one of the tables, where she waited for him to fetch her another drink. He must have adroitly spiked it with the drug, for she had barely had time to consume it when she started to feel what she called 'woozy'. Her companion helped her out and into his car and drove her to an isolated location in New Jersey, where he stripped her, robbed her and burned her breasts with a petrol lighter before throwing her out of his car. She was found lying in the road unconscious by a motorist and rushed to hospital, where she was detained for several days. This victim was able to give police a description of her abductor, but such a description could fit almost any well-turned-out male around thirty, white, about 5ft. 10in. tall, who drove a 'fairly newish-looking dark-coloured car', so the police were no nearer.

A 27-year-old prostitute testified how she was similarly abducted, drugged and brutalized before being thrown out of a car into a vacant lot in Teaneck, New Jersey, where she was found two hours later unconscious, naked, robbed and bleeding from deep bite wounds on her breasts.

While all these indictments were being prepared for his trial and witnesses found and their statements recorded to be put into evidence, Cottingham himself was restive and unstable in custody, making no fewer than four unsuccessful suicide attempts. Eventually, however, he appeared in the Bergen County courtroom in New Jersey to face twenty charges. During one court appearance he managed to elude his guards and make a mad dash down three flights of stairs and out into the street, hotly pursued by half a dozen deputies. Surrounded, he gave up without a struggle, but for further appearances he was fettered.

The jury in the Bergen County Court trial convicted him on fifteen of the twenty indictments; the other five were allowed to remain on file for lack of evidence. He was sentenced to 173 to 197 years in the New Jersey State Penitentiary.

A year later he was returned to the same court to stand trial for the murder of the nurse Maryann Carr two years earlier than his later clutch of crimes. For this he was found guilty of murder in the second degree and was sentenced to twenty-five years to life.

In 1984 Cottingham was brought from the maximum security New Jersey State Prison at Trenton, this time to stand trial in New York for the murder of Deedeh Goodarzi, her unidentified companion and the third prostitute slain in·Manhattan. The trial lasted five weeks. The jury was out only seventy minutes before bringing in a unanimous verdict of second-degree murder in each case. He was given a further seventy-five years to life in prison.

12

Mark of the Vampire

Richard Chase (1978)

The symptoms of a disturbed personality are frequently
exhibited by potential serial murders in their youth. Not
all serial killers-to-be display these symptoms, of course,
but experienced psychiatrists have found this to be so in
an overwhelming majority of cases. Not all the symptoms
are necessarily displayed by any one such individual.

In the case of Richard Chase, who forms the subject of
this chapter, nearly all these symptoms were apparent
very early in his youth, some of them even in his
childhood. Yet over the years that preceded his final
horrific rampage in which he killed six people, all
complete strangers, nobody had considered his bizarre
behaviour as he grew to maturity to be worth bothering
about, and when his behaviour became so over the top
that he was committed to a mental hospital, the doctors
there thought there was nothing really seriously wrong
with him and discharged him with sedative drugs,
enjoining his parents to see that he took the medication
regularly. His mother had other ideas; she thought that

her son did not need to continue with the tablets and, after a few days, started weaning him off them.

A year later, six people, including two little boys, were dead. As a judge was later to agree, none so blind as they who will not see …

Richard Chase was born on 23 May 1950 in Sacramento, California. Up to the age of eight he still wet the bed, and by that age he had started no fewer than four fires in his home. These were attributed to boyish mischief. No advice or counselling from child guidance clinics was sought, or even considered. It was not long before cruelty to animals surfaced in the boy's behaviour. Yet nobody lifted a finger.

Richard attended Mira Loma High School from age fourteen to eighteen. His grades were consistently low. During his sophomore year he notched up an arrest for possession of marijuana, and was ordered to attend a teen work programme on weekends. Later he started taking LSD, and also alcohol. He became progressively more slovenly in his dress and habits, selfish and inconsiderate and openly defiant towards his parents. He was a loner, but occasionally went out on a date with a girl, but quickly found that he was impotent. This blow to his self-esteem had the effect of making him attempt to drown his humiliation in booze.

On leaving high school he entered college, which he treated in the same cavalier fashion as high school, gaining consistently low C grades. On being reprimanded by the college authorities for turning up unkempt, he would retaliate by coming into classes naked. In the spring of 1971 he dropped out – a fellow student said that he would have been expelled anyway.

Just before this time, in February, he had been so frequently on a collision course with his parents that his father ordered him to move out and find a place of his own. The atmosphere in the home had been a constant battleground of wills, culminating in Richard's hitting his mother on the head, yelling, 'You're controlling my mind! Stop it!'

Richard arranged to share an apartment with three fellow-students, agreeing to pay his quarter-share of the rent and utilities. Once he had moved in, he proceeded to board up the door of his room, making a hole in the wall for his entry and exit, saying he had done this to avoid being sneaked up on by his fellow-tenants. They took a very dim view of his eccentric behaviour, as well as a number of other things such as the fact that he was 'stoned up to the eyeballs on drugs' most of the time, did not take any share in the cleaning and cooking, failed to pay his share of the rent, never took a shower and had a very bad case of BO. They also saw him on one occasion waving a handgun out of his window at someone who was outside in the street. They put up with him for three months before asking him to move out. He refused, so they moved out instead. Richard, unable to pay the rent and other outgoings, moved back into his parents' home.

In 1972 his parents separated, and were divorced six months later. One is tempted to surmise that the problems they had with their son was a contributing factor, causing endless rows and bickering between them, the taking of sides often veering wildly for or against the boy in any one of them. The 'boy' was now twenty-two, and theoretically old enough to look after himself, though of course his parents did not seem to realize that he was in no fit state to do so. After the divorce he stayed in his mother's home and his father moved into an apartment a few blocks away. Richard divided his time between them, according to his mood at the time.

His mother must have been relieved when he went to stay with his father from time to time. He used to spend most of the day in bed, never bothering to wash, shave or shower, and his hair grew long and matted. When not in bed or stoned on pot, he was violent, striking his mother, screaming abuse, and on one occasion he tore a door off its hinges.

At about this time Richard began to be obsessed with his physical condition, or rather what he imagined this to be. One night an ambulance arrived, looking for the 'heart attack emergency case'. Shortly after this, he shaved his head, insisting that it was changing shape and that some bones were coming through his skin.

In the house, he was observed frequently to be talking in response to 'voices' which he heard in his head. He would say such things as 'I'm not going to do that' or 'Stop annoying me' when there was no one in the room with him.

In April 1973 he attended a friend's party uninvited and while there made such a nuisance of himself that he was thrown out. After a few minutes he returned, and the host called the police, who arrested the unwelcome gate-crasher. As they did so a .22 calibre revolver fell to the floor from his belt. Taken to jail, he asked his father to bail him out, which he did, and Richard was let off with a caution. The police did not touch him in any way beyond the usual frisking and handcuffing, but he complained that they had badly beaten him up and insisted on being examined by doctors so that he could sue the police. Doctors found no sign of any injury and his father sorted the incident out with the local police chief.

In May he went to live with his grandmother in Los Angeles. If his mother and father were relieved at this respite, the grandmother little knew what she had let herself in for. Besides all the usual talking to imagined voices, lounging about in bed and being constantly stoned on drugs, failing to observe even the most elementary personal hygiene and insisting on eating raw meat, his other bizarre habits also got on her nerves. He used to stand on his head frequently, saying that the blood was draining out of his brain and he needed to replenish it. There was certainly something wrong with his brain, the grandmother thought ... Then there was that walking around the house with his head wrapped in a towel, only his eyes showing. He explained that his head hurt. She offered to take him to the doctor's in her car, but he refused. Eventually she took him to the airport and put him on a plane back to Sacramento.

Shuttling between his mother's house and his father's apartment, neither parent would admit that Richard had major psychiatric problems. His father told him to get himself together, kick the drugs and booze and look for a job. His mother said it was a disturbed personality brought about by his now broken home background, completely ignoring the fact that Richard had exhibited all the signs of mental instability long before the divorce.

On 1 December 1973 Richard walked into the casualty department of the American River Hospital in Sacramento, looking, as the doctors put it, 'wild-looking, foul-smelling, filthy and unkempt', complaining that his head was changing shape and that someone had removed his pulmonary artery and his blood flow had stopped. The doctors in casualty quickly turned him over to the psychiatric ward, where he was given a bath and a change of clothing and was examined by two doctors, who pronounced him to be acutely paranoid caused by drug abuse. They kept him in for observation, sedated owing to his highly agitated state.

Predictably, his mother turned up two days later demanding his release; the doctors reluctantly agreed. She said that the experience of being in a mental ward 'frightened him'.

In the ensuing period, a marked deterioration set in, although his parents would not admit it to themselves. It is interesting to speculate on what grounds they considered that their son was 'making good progress' when he continued to talk to his 'voices', threw food about, spat and swore at them and destroyed furnishings. He also hit his mother during the incessant arguments, and chased visitors from the house with a handgun. On one occasion he knocked a large hole in the wall, and on another tore the telephone from its moorings, wiring included.

By the spring of 1976 Richard's mother had endured enough, although she still refused to admit that there was 'very much wrong' with him. His parents found him a small apartment a few blocks from his mother's home and arranged for him to receive welfare so that he could look after himself. They helped with groceries, laundry and the payment of his utility bills. For a time he seemed calmer, even making a desultory effort to keep himself and the flat clean, although this did not last long before he slipped back into his old habits. Now that he was able to cook for himself, he started to purchase rabbits – but he did not cook them. He disembowelled them and ate them raw, experimenting with various methods of preparing them, including running their viscera together with their blood through a blender. He also drank their blood.

A visit from his father on 26 April 1976 found Richard very ill, shaking uncontrollably and vomiting. He told his father that he had eaten a rabbit which 'must have been going rotten' and had food poisoning. In fact he had injected himself with the blood of a rabbit, but of course his father did not know this.

This bizarre fact was not discovered until after his father had taken him in his car to Sacramento Community Hospital. He had food poisoning, Richard averred, caused by eating a rabbit which had battery acid in its stomach; this had burned through his own stomach. Richard was transferred to the psychiatric wing, where he was diagnosed as a paranoid schizophrenic and sent to the psychiatric unit at American River Hospital. There he admitted what he had done, 'because,' he said, 'his blood was drying up and his body was falling apart, and he needed blood.' After treatment with anti-psychotic drugs, he was thought to have improved sufficiently to be sent to an after-care mental hospital. For once, his mother did not try to get him released. Perhaps she was appreciating the unaccustomed peace and quiet at home.

One day two dead birds, their heads snapped off, were found in the corridor outside Richard's room. When Richard himself appeared, coming in from the grounds, he was covered with blood. He denied all knowledge of the birds, and said he had cut himself when shaving – a statement bizarre in itself considering that Richard had a beard. One day he admitted to an orderly that he had in fact killed the birds and drunk their blood, saying that his own blood was 'draining away' and that he did not want to die.

At the end of September – no more decapitated birds having been found – Richard was discharged to the care of his parents, the diagnosis being 'paranoid schizophrenia, in remission'. The doctors felt that the hospital could not help him further, and that he was not a danger to others, but that it was essential that he continue to take anti-psychotic medication regularly. He was supplied with tablets and a prescription for renewal, and his mother was enjoined to see that he took them.

His parents set him up in another apartment, helping him out as before, and at first his mother saw that he took the drugs. But she was unhappy to see what she called 'the zombie-like state' the tablets kept him in, and gradually reduced them until he was no longer on the drugs.

Predictably, Richard gradually slid into an uncontrolled mental state, during which he told his mother to 'stop controlling his mind' and 'stop trying to poison him'. He said that she was putting dish-washer detergent in his food. His delusions about his own body now reached alarming proportions: he said his heart was getting smaller, his internal organs were moving around inside him, and his stomach was rotting away. He felt that the only way to save his life was to drink blood. He shot cats and dogs, drank their blood, and mixed hellish cocktails of the blood and viscera in his blender. He became reclusive, refusing to admit either of his parents or any of his former friends into his apartment, and going out only at night. Neighbours saw him carrying a shotgun in the street and reported him to the apartment building manager, who told him to cover the gun if he took it outside. Thereafter he wrapped it in a blanket. Dogs and cats, including his mother's two dogs and her cat, disappeared all over the neighbourhood. One day he shot his mother's cat on her own doorstep; when she came out to investigate the noise, Richard was drinking its blood. Still nobody lifted a finger or did a thing; incredibly, not even his mother or the owners of the pets who had fallen to his gun. The stage was set: this human vampire would stop at nothing in his quest.

*   *   *

On 3 August 1977 a car was found stuck in the sand by the shore of Pyramid Lake in Nevada. The interior of the car was smeared with blood, but there was nobody inside. Patrolmen who found the car discovered a .22 calibre rifle and a 30-30 rifle in the car, both bloodstained. There was also a pair of bloody tennis shoes and, to the officers' alarm and horror, a plastic bucket of blood in which there was a liver.

The patrolmen searched the area and some distance away came upon a naked man, covered with blood but apparently uninjured, crouching in a ditch. Asked for his name and address, the man gave it to them: Richard

Chase, giving his mother's address in Sacramento, California. Asked what he was doing in Nevada, he said he was 'on a trip'. He was arrested and the car was impounded for examination. Asked where the blood had come from, he said that it had 'seeped out of his skin'.

Forensic tests determined that the blood – and the liver – had come from a cow. Richard was released, but both his guns were confiscated. He got his car back later after some irregularities in its licensing had been straightened out with the vehicle registration authorities.

Richard's father, who did not even know his son had taken off on a trip, remonstrated with him about using a car with improper registration, and upbraided him for wasting money on a high-powered rifle when the .22 he already had was perfectly adequate for his hunting! One begins to wonder whether Richard's parents were as much out of touch with reality as their son, though in a different way.

Richard was still prowling the neighbourhood for stray cats and dogs, even purchasing dogs from the American SPCA. He was seen taking animals into his apartment on several occasions, but the animals were never seen again. On 2 December he purchased a .22 semi-automatic pistol and several boxes of ammunition. Things seemed to be taking on an ominous look. On 27 December he went cruising around the neighbourhood in his car and took pot shots with his deadly new toy at various targets, mostly derelict buildings, but one shot was fired through a lighted window of an occupied house. Fortunately no one was hurt, but the residents had a nasty shock.

On 29 December Richard went out again. At about 8.30 p.m. he spotted a man walking from his car carrying boxes of groceries into his house, crossing the front garden. Richard fired two shots at him, apparently on impulse. One shot went wide and lodged in a tree; the other hit the man in the chest when he turned round at the sound of the first shot. The man, Ambrose Griffin, died in American River Hospital two hours later.

Police were stymied by the apparently motiveless killing, and were unable to come up with any leads. A car had been seen roaring off afterwards, but it was pitch dark and no one was able to describe either the car or its driver.

In the days that followed, neighbours noticed that Richard had a blank, spaced-out look, not responding to their greetings, looking right through them as though they were not there. They assumed that he was stoned on drugs. Unknown to them, the human time-bomb that was Richard Chase was about to explode.

At 11.45 a.m. on 23 January, Richard went out, his loaded gun, two knives and a pair of rubber gloves concealed under his jacket. His father had previously called on him, but since Richard seemed uncommunicative and did not feel like talking, he left after a few moments. Richard now turned in the direction of a row of houses behind the supermarket. He had to cross the supermarket car park to reach them. In the car park he encountered a neighbour whom he had known for some time, but when she spoke to him he failed to recognize her, saying, 'Who are you?' Frightened by his odd behaviour, she got into her car. As she drove off, he banged on the door of the car with his fist. Later she was to say that 'he seemed like a madman'.

From the car park he walked across the front lawn of one of the houses, where the couple who lived there saw him, and entered a house two doors further along the row, where he had just seen a young woman come outside to empty a waste bin into the garbage can. Unfortunately for her, she had left the door unlocked. Richard fired a shot through the letter box as he entered, whereupon the young woman emerged from a rear room, taking a second shot in the neck. Theresa Wallin, who was twenty-two years old and three months pregnant, fell to the floor, and Richard shot her through the head.

She was still alive, though barely, when her assailant dragged her from the hall, up the stairs and into her bedroom, where he threw her on the bed and tore off her clothes. He then set to work as a crazed butcher. Finding that the two knives he had brought with him were not sharp enough to do the job, he went downstairs to the kitchen and found a sharp-bladed one, which he took with him back to his victim and proceeded to cut her open from just below the neck to the pubic area. He pulled out her intestines, leaving them lying in loops on the floor; then he severed one lung from its moorings, stabbed her liver, cut her diaphragm, sliced her pancreas in half, ripped out her spleen, cut out both her kidneys and laid them on the bed beside her, and finally stabbed her in the heart.

Next he stabbed her through the left nipple repeatedly, smeared her blood over his face and hands, licked it off his fingers, and smeared more of it on her inner thighs. In the room, on a shelf, he found a small plastic cup, from which he drank her blood. Finally he committed upon her the final indignity of urinating and defecating into various orifices of the body.

In the bathroom, he washed all the blood off himself, donned the rubber gloves so as to avoid leaving fingerprints, washed the blood off the knife he had used and replaced it in the kitchen. He apparently failed to notice that he had left smears of blood in the kitchen sink and spots of blood on the knife handle and also on some dishes which were stacked on the draining-board. Then he retrieved his clothes, which he had removed prior to the orgy of mutilation, and left quietly via the rear door and across the back garden, closing the garden gate behind him. No one saw him leave. Neither had anyone heard the three shots he had fired after entering the house; it is assumed that he must have had a silencer on the gun.

The following day (24 January) saw Richard cruising

around a different neighbourhood. He bought copies of all the newspapers, and cut out all the reports of the horrific murder of Theresa Wallin, who had been found by her husband when he came home from work. Richard also called at his mother's house to ask her about going on a picnic, but his mother was not at home, so he spoke to his grandmother, who was later to say that on this visit her grandson appeared perfectly calm and was behaving normally.

The next day the blood lust was upon him again. He cruised around looking for what he considered to be a suitable victim, but failing to find one he shot a dog, which he disembowelled, cutting out its kidneys and eating them raw, and drank its blood. Afterwards he calmly called his mother and they exchanged about twenty minutes' small-talk. She later was to say that she did not think anything was wrong.

On 27 January Richard went out at about 10 a.m. and parked his car near a shopping mall and walked casually along a street of residential houses. He noticed that the front door of one of them had for some reason been left slightly open. Entering the house uninvited, Richard encountered a 27-year-old woman named Evelyn Miroth. Without further ado he shot her in the head.

Even if a gun is fired with a silencer attached, it still makes a soft, muffled plopping sound, and this must have been the noise that summoned Evelyn's son Jason, six years old, from her former marriage, and her boyfriend Daniel Meredith, fifty-two, from the room in which they had been watching television. In the hall, Richard shot Jason, first in the neck and then again in the head. Meredith made towards Richard, who shot him through the head, and a second time when he fell to the ground.

After removing Meredith's wallet and car keys from his pockets Richard dragged the bodies of Evelyn Miroth and Jason upstairs in to the first bedroom he came to, in which he found a 22-month-old baby, Evelyn's nephew David Ferreira, sleeping in his cot. He shot the child at close range, then got to work butchering the body of Evelyn Miroth in very much the same manner as he had done with the body of Theresa Wallin. In addition, he gouged out one of her eyes and left it hanging from its socket. He also sodomized the body, afterwards stabbing it in the rectum. Going downstairs to the kitchen, he found a plastic bucket and a coffee cup for the bloodletting and drinking. This time he did not need to look for a sharp knife; he had brought his own, sharpened to a razor's edge.

Richard next took the baby's body into the bathroom and ran some water in the tub. Immersing the child's body, he dissected the skull, leaving blood and brain tissue in the water. Just at that point, before he had time to do anything else, there was a knock at the door. Peering through the net curtains, he saw that a small neighbourhood girl of about six or so had come, probably to play with Jason. She waited for a little while, but obtaining no response, she went home again. When her mother tried to call the house, there was no reply. Richard now thought it best to leave. After all, the child's mother could come in person to investigate. Hastily washing the blood from his body and throwing on the clothes he had left over a chair, he grabbed a large plastic bag he found in the bathroom, probably a laundry bag, and put the baby's body into it. No one saw him leave the house, carrying the bag, and get into Meredith's red Ford estate car and drive off. He parked in a vacant lot not far from his apartment, and somehow managed to return home, carrying the child's body without anyone at all seeing him. Leaving the body there, still in its bag, Richard then went back to retrieve his own car.

Back in his apartment, the human vampire decapitated the body, drank the blood and consumed the brain. He then carried out the most horrific mutilations, opening the body and removing several organs. After collecting more blood to be drunk later, he stuffed what was left of the remains into a plastic bag and put it in a cardboard box on the floor.

*   *   *

That afternoon, just as Richard had feared, the mother of the little girl who had been Jason's playmate called at the house. It was quite unusual for her friends not to be at home at that time of day. She thought that perhaps something might be amiss, such as illness. But nothing could have prepared her for the grisly discoveries she made when she entered the still unlocked front door. The house was a shambles, with blood everywhere, and the killer's bloody footprints all over the hall, stairs, kitchen, bathroom and one bedroom. Stepping over the fully clothed bodies of Jason Miroth and Daniel Meredith, the woman made her way fearfully up the stairs, heedless of whether the homicidal intruder might be still in the house. When she saw the nude, mutilated body of her friend lying on the bed, and the blood-drenched empty cot where David usually slept, she dashed screaming from the house.

Police were certain that the missing child had been killed, owing to the quantity of blood in and around his cot, and also because they found a .22 calibre slug embedded in the pillow. In the bath water they found brain tissue, blood and faeces, which subsequent forensic examination was able to prove were those of a small child. Faeces found on the floor and also on the bed on which Evelyn's brutalized body lay were proved to have come from an adult.

While technicians were dusting for prints, scraping up various samples and photographing the scene of the carnage and eventually removing the bodies to the morgue, the police were pulling out all the stops in an intensive door-to-door canvass of the entire area in the vicinity of the house. The woman who had found the bodies was in shock and had been taken to hospital, where she was kept under sedation and was unable to give a coherent account to the police for several days.

The following day the dragnet included the block in which Richard's apartment was situated. When officers knocked on his door, he was lying on his bed avidly reading the accounts of the murder in the various newspapers. He kept quiet and did not respond to the knock. A little later they were back, having received a lead from a neighbour that there was definitely someone in his apartment as she had heard somebody moving about.

The three detectives bided their time, and their patience was rewarded. The neighbour had been right: there *was* someone at home, they could hear movement quite plainly. The three detectives looked at one another: now why would someone not respond to a knock? The officers pounded on the door. 'Police! Open up!'

The door opened, and Richard confronted them, holding a large cardboard box. He tried to retreat into his apartment and slam the door, but an officer prevented him. Richard then tried to sidestep the officer and run out, but another policeman was blocking his way of escape. Richard flung the box at the officer and dived under the policeman's legs in a flying rugby tackle, but the three men easily subdued him after a short scuffle and handcuffed him. The cardboard box flew open as Richard threw it, and the officers were horrified at seeing its contents: bloody rags, a plastic cup which had contained blood, a child's diaper and pin, and pieces of brain tissue and bone.

The officers entered the apartment to look for the missing child while Richard sat with other detectives in the car. They did not find the child, but they were appalled at the condition of the apartment. The entire flat was covered with bloodstains and splashes from floor to ceiling, on walls and furniture, bedding and clothes, even the newspapers he had been reading. The bath tub was half-full of bloody water. There were faeces on the floor in the bedroom. The kitchen was awash with blood, and there were cups and glasses containing, or which had contained, blood. Towels were bloody, and there were bones scattered about. The stench was indescribable.

The detectives left the building just as quickly as they possibly could, took Richard to the police station, and rushed through an application for a search warrant, alerting forensic specialists to be prepared for a few shocks. On being searched, his automatic pistol, in a shoulder holster, was removed; it was fully loaded and the safety catch was off. In his pockets were found boxes of .22 slugs, two knives, a pair of rubber gloves, and a wallet containing Daniel Meredith's credit cards and 77 dollars in cash. The suspect told police he had found Meredith's wallet in a parking lot.

'Let me go!' Richard said. 'I haven't done anything. I just killed a dog, that's all!'

'With all that blood, the dog must have been the size of an elephant!' one officer rejoined sarcastically.

'I shot a few dogs, that's all!' the suspect insisted. 'Now will you let me go?'

'Where is the child?'

'What child? I don't know anything about any child. I just killed some dogs, that's all.' The suspect continued to deny all knowledge of the crime. He admitted that he had drunk the blood of dogs and eaten their viscera, but that was as far as he went. He also stoutly maintained that he had found Meredith's wallet in a car park nearby.

The forensic team sent to evaluate the suspect's apartment were not just shocked – they were horrified beyond anything they had encountered before. The woman member of the team vomited on the spot, then quickly left and asked the station superintendent to send a male replacement. Two men who were part of the examination team also vomited. The odour of blood and decomposition was horrific enough, but in the kitchen they found a dinner plate containing a slab of fresh brain tissue swimming in blood, and it was almost in fear and trepidation that they opened the door of the freezer. Their fears were justified when they examined a large freezer container, in which were assorted visceral organs, some human, some animal. The refrigerator was so arranged that the shelves would accommodate large items. A bloody machete was found in a drawer of the kitchen cabinet. Slugs of .22 calibre lay on the floor, and there were bullet holes in the ceiling and in the woodwork, implying that these had been used for target practice. Pinned to the wall were several lurid pictures of human internal organs which had apparently been cut from a medical book. The book was found, minus several pages, on a shelf in the main room of the apartment. Curiously, no books were found dealing with cannibalism, vampirism, sado-masochism or the like. Only gun magazines seemed to have any bearing on the suspect's proclivities; the other books were innocuous enough, such as any young man might own. His high school yearbooks had been kept, and at the end of the shelf was a brown manila envelope containing a bundle of newspaper cuttings of not only this latest outrage but also the Theresa Wallin killing, the shooting of Ambrose Griffin, and sundry break-in offences, in which an intruder had been reported but nothing stolen. In one case after leaving rooms in disarray, the intruder had urinated into an opened drawer of clothes, and defecated on a child's bed. In all these cases the houses he had broken into were unoccupied at the time. Police theorized that the vandalism had been triggered by frustration at finding no one at home as a potential victim to sate his bloodlust.

Under intensive interrogation at the police station, Richard repeatedly denied any involvement in the hideous outrages, admitting only to killing a number of dogs. Confronted with material evidence, including the contents of the box he had thrown at a police officer when trying to escape capture, he still insisted that the blood and other material found had come from dogs. When asked why he had attempted to avoid apprehension, he replied that he did not know who was banging on his door and thought that it might be the building manager complaining about the dogs barking. Asked about the organs in his freezer, he replied that it was all dog meat. He said that he liked to eat dog meat, adding, 'They do that in China, you know.'

'Well, this isn't China – it's the good old USA!' the interrogating officer countered shortly. 'And I don't believe you. Those organs in your freezer are human.'

'You're crazy!' Richard replied. 'Are you trying to say I'm a cannibal? It's dog meat, I tell you. Human organs? No way. That's not my bag.'

The next day Richard was cautioned, advised of his Miranda rights, and interviewed by two psychiatrists appointed by the DA's office. At first he refused to talk to them, but later changed his mind. Now he decided to admit to his crimes, and the story he was to tell them had them paling beneath their tans.

Describing his crimes in a detached, emotionless manner, Richard showed no remorse or guilt. 'I had to do what I did,' his confession ran. 'I have blood poisoning which is slowly draining the blood from my body and I need blood all the time to replace it or I would die. I was fed up with hunting animals for this purpose, and after thinking about it for some time I decided to kill humans for their blood.

'I killed the first one when I saw a lady out front of her house ... I followed her into her house. She had left the door unlocked ...'

'Would you have broken in if she had locked the door?' the psychiatrist asked.

'No, I don't think so,' the prisoner replied. 'I would have looked for someone else.'

'What did you do then?'

'As soon as I was in the house I saw the lady. I shot her in the head. She fell to the floor. I started stabbing and cutting her, and I drank some of her blood.'

After describing in detail the brutalities he inflicted on Theresa Wallin, Richard was asked to describe what he had done at the Miroth home.

'I was walking around like before ... I found another house with the door unlocked. I just walked in, and a lady came into the hall and screamed, so I shot her in the head. As she fell down, a guy came running out of another room. He rushed toward me and was going to try to grab my gun, so I let him have it ...'

'You mean you shot him?'

'Yeah. I shot him in the head, same as the lady. Then I saw a boy, six or seven, something like that. He was just standing there looking scared. I just shot him, too. It all happened so fast ...'

'What did you do then, now that you had killed three people?'

'I heard a baby crying upstairs, so I went up there. It was hollering so much, making so much noise, that I shot it too to shut it up. Then I went downstairs and carried the lady up and laid her on the bed and started stabbing and cutting her ...'

After describing the grisly mutilations, the prisoner described how he took the baby from its cot and carried it home when he left the house:

I was going to dissect it in the bath, but then I heard someone at the front door. I peeked out and saw it was some neighbourhood kid. So I thought I'd better leave. I put the baby's body in a laundry bag I found in the bathroom. I took a red car which was parked outside so I could get home without being seen. Then I left the car in a vacant lot and went and fetched my own car from the supermarket car park where I'd left it. The red car must have belonged to the guy in the house, because his keys fitted it. When I got home I removed the brains to eat later, and I drank some of the blood.

The decomposed remains of the child, together with its clothing and Meredith's car keys, were found about eight weeks later, wedged into a small cardboard supermarket carton, dumped in a vacant lot. From the position of the box, it appeared to have been thrown over a fence.

Subsequently Richard was interviewed by the Assistant DA, who asked him to elucidate several other points which had not been included in his confession. Asked why he had shot Ambrose Griffin, he denied that it was just target practice. He said that Nazi Germans were living in the Ambrose house and issuing threats to him over the airwaves. He was then questioned about the dogs he had killed. He said that he rounded up strays, stole a few, and the rest he purchased through advertisements of dogs in the newspapers for sale, or offered free to good homes.

'How many dogs do you think you killed?'

'Oh, about twenty-five, I think.' Gratuitously he added that he hanged two of them before he purchased his gun.

Richard steadfastly refused to tell his interrogator where he had disposed of the baby's remains. But he returned to the subject of his animal slaughter. In addition to the estimated twenty-five dogs, he admitted killing at least twenty cats, numerous rabbits and assorted birds, and two cows. One of these latter must have been the one whose liver and blood had been removed near Pyramid Lake in Nevada, but its body was never found. It must be assumed that its owner discovered it and had the carcass destroyed or, if found soon enough, butchered for meat.

Richard was then asked to recount once again in full detail his killings and subsequent brutalities in the Wallin and Miroth homes, which he did. The Assistant DA was visibly shocked by the prisoner's matter-of-fact description of his hideous crimes.

Meanwhile, police removed just about everything from Richard's apartment: furniture, kitchen appliances, carpets, clothing, television set, books – the lot. Among his belongings a notebook was discovered, containing many evidences of a disordered mind, including lists of people he thought were conspiring against him. This list included several well-known stars and celebrities. The entries in the notebook were disjointed and bore no relation to one another, nor were they dated in diary form. Some of the entries were in German, and there was also a list of words in English with their translations into German. He had also written on one page, in English and German, 'I will end the world by flooding if I get killed.'

Asked questions which related to his paranoid delusions of persecution, he replied, 'There seems to be enough evidence to prove that I'm not suffering from delusions of persecution, but that I am really being persecuted'. He insisted that his mother had tried to poison him by putting dishwasher detergent in his food.

In prison, Richard's delusions about his food being poisoned continued. He blamed the 'screws' who were 'putting volatile acid and venereal disease' in his rations. He said that this was the result of a conspiracy against him by prison guards. He was convinced that his body was deteriorating still further owing to the lack of blood, and demanded that he be given blood transfusions. He also pestered the guards to obtain animal blood for him to drink from the kitchen where meat was prepared. When naturally they refused his bizarre requests, he shouted abuse at them. He was a most recalcitrant prisoner, refusing to flush his toilet after use, spitting at guards, refusing to wash or shave, and screaming to be let out of jail, often in the middle of the night, waking other inmates. He refused to associate with other prisoners, averring that they were all Nazis who were persecuting him because he was Jewish. Richard Chase was not Jewish. It was just another of his paranoid delusions.

A whole battery of eminent psychiatrists assessed Richard to decide whether he was sane or insane in law. Inevitably there were disagreements. On the side for insanity they understandably asserted that he was as mad as a hatter and that only a complete madman could have carried out such frightful deeds. On the other side, however, they cited premeditation, malice aforethought and the knowledge that what he was doing was wrong, pointing out that the prisoner had gone out looking for a victim, carrying a gun, knives and other accoutrements, and that he had consciously avoided being seen either entering or leaving the houses where he had committed the murders. In the case of the shooting of Ambrose Griffin, he had sped off in his car immediately afterwards. After a child from the neighbourhood had knocked at the door of the Miroth home, he had precipitately left the premises. That, the psychiatrists said, negated insanity in law, although they were the first to admit that the prisoner was clearly a disturbed person with mental aberrations of major proportions, including paranoid schizophrenia. That, however, did not prevent him from knowing the nature and quality of his acts – to quote the M'Naghten Rules – and knowing that what he was doing was wrong.

Largely on account of this conflicting psychiatric testimony, the DA fell back on the ace card that he was playing close to his chest. This was his contention that the Ambrose Griffin killing was not, as the accused said, a manifestation of his bizarre paranoid delusion that Nazis were there and threatening him, but purely and simply target practice – a trial run, as it were. This was substantiated by the fact that bullet holes were found in the ceiling and woodwork in his apartment. He had to feel confident that he was able to use his recently acquired gun properly. He was by no means a particularly good shot, as was demonstrated by the fact that several of his victims had been shot more than once.

Unfortunately, all the bullets that had been recovered from his victims' bodies, as well as those found in the ceiling and timbers at the flat, were distorted or warped, and could not be matched to Richard's gun. The police then had a lucky break. A man came forward to tell them that one night he had heard shots, which at the time he had thought to be a car backfiring. Some days later he had gone into his basement store when he noticed that some wooden panelling was curiously warped. On closer examination he observed that this had been caused by a .22 bullet that had been shot into it from a distance. He brought the bullet to the police, who were able to make a perfect match with Richard's gun. The DA was elated – this was yet further evidence that Richard had been out practising – in other words, a premeditated act.

* * *

As the date of the trial drew near, a change of venue was sought, and obtained, by the defence, on the grounds that feelings were running so high in Sacramento that the accused's trial would be prejudiced. It would also be difficult to find prospective jurors who were unbiased. The trial was transferred to San José. It probably did little to influence the proceedings, however, for media coverage had been so great that the case was common knowledge not only throughout California but in every other state in the Union.

Richard Chase was charged with six counts of murder in the first degree. Ronald Tochterman, the Assistant District

Attorney in charge of the prosecution, was determined that Richard would not be allowed to get away with an insanity verdict. Tochterman, now a superior court judge, was a formidable prosecutor with a reputation for thoroughness and the courage of his convictions, if I may coin a phrase. He was well-prepared for all the arguments the defence could conceivably throw at him. It was the burden of the prosecution to prove beyond all reasonable doubt that the accused had acted with premeditation, deliberation and malice aforethought.

The defence was quick to capitalize on the opinion of several psychiatrists that Richard Chase was so completely and utterly dominated by his unnatural need for human blood that he was devoid of any ability to perceive that his actions, taken to satisfy that need, were wrong and contrary to law. Tochterman outlined his opposing view with clarity, pointing out that Chase's actions had not been wild, uncontrolled or haphazard but, on the contrary, were all committed with great deliberation. His premeditation was demonstrated by his having practised using his gun, by going out equipped not only with a gun but with knives and rubber gloves – the latter for the express purpose of avoiding leaving incriminating fingerprints – and by going out looking for victims. He also avoided being seen entering or leaving the scenes of his crimes. 'If that is not knowing that what he had done was wrong and against the law,' Tochterman said forcefully, 'then what is it?' An insane man, he averred, would not have made any effort to avoid being apprehended by the police.

The prosecutor had yet another trump card to play. He pointed out the element of progression in Chase's behaviour: first he purchased the gun, then he practised using it. After that, he shot a man from a distance, as if to test his newly acquired skills; then, finally, he shot his victims from a few feet away. 'No!' thundered Tochterman. 'That is not the action of a madman. That is premeditation, deliberation and malice aforethought!'

Further evidence of progression in Chase's behaviour was shown by his having started by killing small animals such as rabbits and birds, then graduating to larger ones, such as cats and dogs, and after that, cows. Finally, he killed humans to obtain the blood he felt he needed.

Tochterman's powerful arguments won the day. The jury after only a short deliberation found Richard Chase guilty on all six counts of first-degree murder: Ambrose Griffin, Theresa Wallin, Evelyn Miroth, Jason Miroth, Daniel Meredith and David Ferreira had been avenged. Chase was sentenced to death. He had been adjudged sane in the eyes of the law.

Richard was sent to death row in San Quentin. His behaviour was so bizarre and erratic that he was transferred temporarily to the state mental hospital at Vacaville, where he was put on a course of medication. He had been more than the prison guards could cope with, demanding fresh human or animal blood and screaming and shouting abuse at guards when naturally his demented requests could not be met. When he had calmed down somewhat he was returned to the prison and officers were enjoined to ensure that he took his prescribed drugs regularly.

On death row, Richard kept to himself and refused to fraternize with other inmates. In the meantime, his sentence was appealed. Under Californian state law, all death sentences are appealed automatically, whether the prisoner wishes it or not. Very few do not.

Richard became more and more depressed in prison. Some take the view that the depression was caused by his inability to obtain blood – a frustration that was still able to filter through to his conscious mind despite the massive doses of anti-psychotic medication that the guards saw to it that he took regularly as prescribed. Other sources have been quoted as thinking that he was not deeply depressed but in fact was anxious to cure himself and that to this end he began saving up some of his tablets and hoarding them until such time as he could take an excessive dose at one time, in the belief that this would cure him of the delusion that was destroying his peace of mind. After some time, prison guards, considering that he could now be trusted to take the tablets at the appointed times without their supervision, failed to watch him take them and ensure that he did so. They had doubtless been lulled into a state of false security – or, quite possibly, they just became slapdash at the job.

Either way, one day Richard raided his stock of tablets and took the lot. On Christmas Eve 1979, he was found dead in his cell. The doctors were not a little surprised, because never at any time during his numerous interviews had he ever expressed any suicidal intent or feelings, and during his life before his imprisonment he had never likewise been known to harbour suicidal feelings.

Yet another opinion voiced at the time was that he *was* depressed and that he had taken the overdose at a time of mental fuzziness caused by the drugs, possibly waking and taking them in the half-awake, half-asleep state that sometimes causes people to think they have forgotten to take their medication and take it again. Still, if that had been the case, it still would not explain why he took a large quantity of tablets, not just the one or two he was accustomed to taking at one time.

No, I do not go along with any of these theories – all conveniently postulated in various quarters to fit Richard Chase into a suitable cubby-hole of behaviour motivation. In my personal opinion, Richard Chase committed suicide. It was as simple as that. Hoarding quantities of tablets over a period was a deliberate, premeditated act. And killing himself was malice aforethought. As it was argued in court between the expert witnesses at the trial, a person can be insane, psychotic, completely dominated by paranoid delusions, but can still be aware of the consequences of his actions, and know the nature and quality of them. In other words, such a person can know that they are wrong and contrary to law.

Why did he commit suicide? Depression? Maybe. But uppermost in his deranged mind was the knowledge that in prison he would never be able to obtain fresh human, or even animal, blood. In his obsessed mind's disordered depths, he knew that he would never be able to sustain this frustration over the long period of his incarceration on death row pending the protracted appeal formalities. So he chose the easy way out.

What I find most amazing is the almost total indifference to his condition shown by nearly everyone who was in contact with him. Various members of his family, who had a better opportunity than anyone else, were confronted with the most bizarre and abnormal manifestations of his mental instability from early childhood, yet they consistently and, one could say, almost resolutely blindfolded their eyes against seeing and realizing that anything was wrong, and had ample warnings of the way things were going. At school and college, both his teachers and his fellow students saw him just as a somewhat extreme but harmless eccentric.

Police at the Nevada lake location, incredibly, just let him go with a citation for an improperly licensed car. Doctors at the mental hospital wards, where he had been conveniently dumped out of the way when he got a bit too obstreperous for his family's comfort, admitted that he was disturbed but considered him not to be a danger to others. On being discharged with medication to keep him in a controlled state, his mother actively set about stopping him taking the tablets. His father was perfectly aware that his unstable son possessed two guns.

Even his neighbours could not fail to observe behaviour on his part that classified him immediately as a 'weirdo', as many of them came forward to testify at his trial.

Long before tragedy overtook Ambrose Griffin, Theresa Wallin, the Miroths, Daniel Meredith and an innocent baby, Richard Chase could have been stopped in his tracks. A panel of doctors from, say, a high-security mental hospital such as Atascadero (equivalent to our Broadmoor) would only have had to talk to him for an hour or so about his killings of rabbits, cats, dogs, birds and cows and imbibing their blood, eating their viscera raw and injecting himself with rabbit blood, in order to certify him as a dangerous psychotic who was liable in a very short time to escalate his bloodletting to include humans. In Atascadero or some similar facility, he would have been no danger to society.

What is society? It is the parents, the grandmothers, the teachers, the students, the friends, the neighbours. It is the police, the doctors, the courts. Society is everyone who bears some responsibility for their fellow men. Society is *us*.